in
the
service
of
11:11

in
the
service
of
11:11

by

George Mathieu Barnard

A Celestial / Mortal Alliance

11.11
Publishers

Australia

Pictured on the cover: "Clearing Skies"
by John de Koster of the Netherlands.

11.11 Publishers
Australia

1111angels.com
1111ProgressGroup.com

© George Mathieu Barnard, 2010
Cover layout: John de Koster
Cover design: Terry Clark
Interior design and production: Terry Clark

First published on CD-ROM by 11.11 Publishers Pty Ltd, 2000
Re-published in Print on Demand by 11.11 Publishers Pty Ltd, 2004

National Library of Australia Cataloging-in-Publication

Barnard, George Mathieu
    In the service of 11:11: a celestial / mortal alliance
    / George Barnard.— 2nd ed.

ISBN 978-0-9577889-5-4

1. Guardian angels. 2. Guides (Spiritualism).

I. Title.

(Series: 11:11 documents)

133.9

Printed in the United States of America
by Bookmasters Distribution of Ohio
10 9 8 7 6 5 4 3 2 1

To
Sandra, Judy A, Geoff, Heather and Alex, Judy M,
Nelson, Loyda, Véronique L, Véronique H, Eveline, Philippe,
Cristina, Vera, John, Marlene, Susan and Conway,
Greg, Mahsa, Petra, Lynn, Simon, Anne,
Lilly, Sarah, Michelle, Andy,
Jeanene, Terry, and Debra.
Special recognition to Paul.

Your support in getting this
book to press and your
contributions to the 11:11
Progress Group and its many
activities have been of great value.

*In loving memory of Carol Asha."

Disclaimer

Some names and locations have been altered to protect family, friends, and patients.

Claimer

For those who like the unexpected: There is humor and sadness—an insight into the hectic life, challenges, and emotions of an industrialist-therapist-student-husband-father-psychic healer . . . all rolled into one. Experience an escape with this mortal rookie, George Mathieu Barnard, into another reality—another dimension of time—and for a time.

For those who study human behavior: Meet the "Characters."

For those who modify human behavior: Here are a number of approaches, as well as wild—and not so wild—theories about the anatomy of the human mind, spirit, and soul . . . and Time.

For those who are searching for a more spiritual life: Here is one way of doing it.

And for those who rightly call themselves illumined, relate to the Light, call themselves Urantians, are graduates of the Great Master's Golden Flame—and even those who suspect "that seagull" might not be a bird: Meet some of your distant cousins, the 1,111 Spirit Guardians of the Temporal Halfway Realm (and others) in multidimensional time, and enjoy learning about the projects of this unique Celestial-Mortal Alliance.

CONTENTS

Celestial Foreword

This book is a unique account of a mortal's willingness to cooperate with the Celestial Servants that are created for the sole purpose of serving the countless generations of their distant mortal relatives. We are the Spirit Guardians, the Planetary Helpers, the Natives of the Temporal Halfway Realm, who make it our task to assist you as individuals and as a species in your evolution-ary climb to become God-knowing sons and daughters of the Creator Parent of us all. I am the long-time leader of the 11:11 Emergency Platoon about which this writing tells.

I am ABC-22.

Midwayer Chief, ABC-22 (nicknamed Bzutu) joined the Red Man who long ago traveled over the Bering Straits onto the American continents before rising ocean levels inundated that land tongue, and divided the Americas from the Eurasian landmass; separating for good the red and yellow races.

The 37-thousand-year-old Warrior, Chief, Shaman and Teacher, was for countless generations the Planetary Helper of the Kiowa Comanche. With the decline in the numbers of the red tribes he was posted to Australia to head the 11:11 Emergency Platoon.

All Midwayers, as well as their Seraphic Superiors, have numbers or alphabetical/numerical codes. The rela-tively few with open human contact frequently have names as well as codes.

Bzutu's presence is often made known at 1:22 AM or PM, in all time zones across the globe. Presently he is in charge of some dozen or more Midwayer Helpers that have arrived from other planets to assist us in this new age called the Correcting Time.

Author's Preface

Now that I am in my sixties, I can look back over a lifetime of frequent verbal and visual contact with celestial beings—the kind I describe in this book. When I was only six years of age, I thought them to be human visitors. They often arrived at meal times and I presumed they waited around until the meal was over to speak to my father about political matters. At that time, the most frequent visitor was MNO-8, or Dr. Mendoza. He often came to visit and would stand between my mom and dad at the opposite end of the table. I only thought of him as "the man who ate no dinners," but I had no idea that, of the eight other members in my family, not one could see the visitor.

All throughout my teenage years, I received advice from these beings, and because their advice was always positive, I came to rely on them as close friends, calling them my Spirit Guides. Not until my 32nd year, at the time when I opened my clinic, did I finally catch sight of these Spirit Guides. Since they looked just like humans, I at first believed them to be ghosts. They appeared to be too young to have been around for as long as they claimed to have been. During the following three decades, they showed themselves somewhat less often, but I became intuitively aware of their appearance.

Frequently, also, they would prompt me to check the time at 11:11 am or wake me at 11:11 pm. These time prompts meant they were "uploading" some data into my deeper conscious mind, and this information would later surface at the precise time it was needed.

To take care of a young family, run a business, as well as a clinic is an awesome task, but I could always count on the help of the Spirit Guardians. They would assist with advice in business as well as with valid suggestions in a clinical environment. It was obvious that their prime concern was with my patients, many of which were trauma cases, while some were even suicidal. And, logically, for me to be able to spend adequate time with the patients, the business needed to run smoothly, and therefore some worthwhile contracts as well as the best of skilled workers were made to come my way.

For almost four decades I worked with my Spirit Guardian family, certain there were other human contact personalities on the planet. Not until quite recently, and as I placed my books "out there," did I meet up with others who had a working relationship with the 1,111 Spirit Guardians. During all those years of celestial-mortal cooperation we were a relatively isolated group of workers. We were "regulars" who got to understand each other, respect each other, admire each other, and indeed love each other, although we were different species, creatures of different origins, and, presumably, personalities with different destinies.

The leader of the 11:11 Emergency Platoon, ABC-22, tended to be the first to arrive when needed. Responsible for the activities of quite a few others, he was always undeniably businesslike. Simone, also known as Sharmon, or MNO-6, was our lightning-fast messenger. Lighthearted and carefree, she would often surprise me, frequently imitate me, or assure me she was one of the flashiest dressers of the Midway Realm.

Simone would clown around, get to the point, and then depart as swiftly as she arrived.

Andrea, a more time-distant, androgynous entity, would always be present, but "she" would rarely be visible. My apprehension about the Creator producing offspring that were both male and female is what at first produced my apprehension about her. It was certainly my problem, not Andrea's. She considered "herself" to be a virgin and servant of the Gods. MNO-8, or Dr. Mendoza, specialized in helping me with the patients. It took me some months to realize that whenever we were on an out-of-body trip, it was Dr. Mendoza who generally promoted these forays into the Midway Realm. This writing covers a number of those unusual healings, when, rather than working at a great distance; I was actually transported to the spot.

During these years of cooperation there were other occasional celestial visitors. There was the occasional Seraph who made her presence known. A Melchizedek materialized in my clinic with an important message when I was searching for one of my Spirit Guides. At one time a creature called a Companion turned up. He was small and cute, but hardly a toy. He was a brilliant linguist and ancient wise one. It soon became clear that the 11:11 Emergency Platoon was but a tiny clan in an enormous universal organization for progress.

The chapters in this book contain some important events of the past five decades. They are so laid out as to give you a clear impression of the kind of work a celestial-mortal progress group of this planet will experience.

If you yearn for a more rewarding, more spiritual existence, be aware of the Spirit Guardians' 11:11 digital prompts on your clocks, VCRs, microwave ovens. The brilliantly minded 11:11 Spirit Guardians are seeking worldwide human involvement for their task of promoting planetary progress and greater spiritual awareness.

Perhaps you will join a Celestial-Mortal Alliance for the benefit of all, and this writing will then greatly assist you, for truly, no one should ever again be so "thrown off the deep end" and waste so much of the Spirit Guardians' time as did the Spirit Guardians' rookie student, George Barnard.

Apologies to the Guardians

"For all the sick jokes I ever told you,
    forgive me for wasting your valuable time.

For all the bird-brained projects I ever dreamed up,
    your pet vertebrate is truly sorry, too.

For every time I questioned your integrity,
    please accept my heart-felt apologies.

And for all the dumb questions I insisted on asking,
    remember I am only the basest, yet most complex,
    of all His creatures.

One puzzling question still remains to be asked:
Why pick on me for this awesome task?"

part one

A Celestial / Mortal Alliance

It had taken George Mathieu Barnard more than a decade to finally make visual contact with the 11:11 Spirit Guardians of the Halfway Realm. As a child, "petit George" often noticed their presence, and as an adult he freely talked to them, sometimes receiving an appropriate response from the Guardians. Most often, advice and warnings were simply implanted in the mortal's mind as he slept. He would awaken with remarkably accurate knowledge of future events. Barnard learned to trust this knowledge, and he acted on it with much success.

Visual contact with the 11:11 was probably in part due to his having fluked the deepest of near-death meditation levels. His consistent requests to be permitted to deal with them on a personal level, he suspects, made the Spirit Guardians decide to relent, for they finally showed themselves. Coming face-to-face with the Warrior ABC-22, the androgynous Andréa, and Juliette the Seraph, quickly strengthened the bonds of true friendship between the mortal and his until-recently-hidden Superiors. The Guardians became his most trusted comrades.

Alas, Barnard now expected the Celestial /

Mortal Alliance for progress to become much more successful. That was presumptuous of him. He was ever so wrong. An over-eagerness to please, especially on the part of the mortal, became the cause of a great many misunderstandings between them. There seemed to be nothing more easily misconstrued than the spoken word, no one as deaf as a human with two perfectly good ears, and nothing as deadly as Barnard's false pride.

1

The Androgynous Guardian

At times, his Spirit Superiors simply didn't have the answer to what he wished to know. Sometimes they admitted to having been specifically instructed not to answer the rookie's more searching questions. Often there were instances when things could pan out in two or more ways, and even to the Guardians' advanced level of cosmic insight, the future was then considered as yet indeterminate.

On top of that, their "code of conduct manual" of rules, or ethics, contained a horrific number of standard limitations when dealing with their much-loved, but only passably intelligent evolutionary pet creatures.

Lately it had become almost a certainty that the Eleven-Eleven were still further restrained in the extent to which they could transmit information. They frequently dealt with phenomena their flesh-and-blood student could not possibly comprehend. Amongst each other they casually communicated at high speed in concepts Barnard could not begin to wrap his mortal mind around. And in these situations he inevitably misunderstood the Guardians.

Barnard decided he should be more careful. But curiosity, stubbornness, a need for adventure and a lack of fear, would get him into trouble.

The Spirit Guardians could not always be on hand to protect him.

Both Andréa and the Seraph Juliette might perhaps be around, but the mortal could not perceive them. The Warrior seemed to be quite alone. Casually leaning on his spear, he stood no more than a few paces from the rookie. This was not a happy-looking Spirit Guardian, and his eyes conveyed a message of shame, embarrassment, even guilt that George Mathieu should be feeling.

The human felt no shame, no embarrassment. And the non-productive need to feel useless guilt of any kind had long ago been dispensed with. Barnard waited.

"You may not belong to a cult," sounded ABC-22's command. Here, it seemed, was his immediate Superior's first ever attack on the mortal's legitimacy of franchise to determine his own actions. It surprised and upset Barnard to be so bluntly directed.

"So, what have I done?" the rookie questioned sharply. "They are a harmless bunch of Christian freaks, Bzutu. I'm only investigating this crowd. I might actually learn something useful."

"You may not belong to a cult!" the Guardian loudly insisted.

"I heard you the first time," Barnard mumbled under his breath as the majestic Warrior and his mighty weapon slowly faded from view. The Guardian had upset his friend. The pig-headed underling returned to visit the cult, just one more time.

It turned out to be one time too many.

Shortly after that evening's "prayer meeting," another visitor who claimed to have been a devotee of Satan, subjected Barnard to an excruciatingly painful psychic attack.

For an hour at least, Barnard was in great pain. And for more than a week he felt emotionally undone by the attack. ABC-22's subsequent explanation of what had really happened to his mortal student made no sense whatever to George Mathieu. The Guardian and his human charge were having serious communication difficulties, no doubt of that.

Optimistic by nature, Barnard tended to put too much trust in his luck wherever he went. Though far from dense, the multi-lingual George Mathieu still lacked the conceptual expertise to fully grasp the vastly superior mind-to-mind concepts of the Halfway Realm. He had made up his mind. "You call me," he light-heartedly suggested to the Guardians. "Ah ain't gonna call you no more."

If the Guardians weren't about, some Seraph would be, and she would soon pass the message on to them.

Seraphim are unbelievable chatterboxes and they love to comply.

The annual holidays were practically upon them, just weeks away. Barnard had some patients' treatments to complete before Christmas, which would allow him to depart with a clean slate, as far as it concerned the clinic.

In an effort to ensure all workers could enjoy their extended break, and for his factory to be closed for the period, much overtime had been allocated. One might be forgiven for thinking the place was starting to resemble an asylum for the mentally troubled. The pressure was on, and tempers were running hot at times—a mediator's night terror.

Together with his wife, Jodi, George would visit Manila and Baguio City in the Philippines. They planned to visit some friends, healers of renown. Then the couple would spend the rest of their three weeks in Bali for an urgently needed rest, perhaps some diving on the coral reefs.

Their children would stay in Australia. The three would surely miss their parents, but they would have each other. The children knew the family they would be with staying with. They often played with this couple's children, and the little Barnards were looking forward to travelling to a faraway "really, really, real farm" in the West, not a make-believe farm, like their own few hundred acres of forest on the outskirts of the town.

George Mathieu was vaguely uneasy, though not overly troubled about leaving his three busybodies behind. Jodi was the one who needed the break from the children's constant demands. All three were so very lively. Jodi looked fatigued, pinched, plumb out of energy. Their last real holiday was years ago, now a distant memory.

But something important was brewing. There had been almost a week of regular 11:11 PM courtesy wake-up calls, as well as a few 11:11 reminders during the day. It seemed Barnard might have to take care of something mighty troublesome, even before they could board their plane in three weeks time.

The rookie could wait no more. He needed to ask the Spirit Guardians what was going to happen.

No sooner had he dived into a deep trance, taking only seconds to reach that tranquil state, than the mighty Warrior was by his side, almost within reach and clear as day on the screen of his mind.

"I made you all a promise I would give you a lengthy break, Bzutu," he told the Guardian. "But you know how fickle we vertebrates are. We have the very best of intentions, but then we change our frivolous minds. Fear is what motivates us."

It had never been one of ABC-22's assignments to acknowledge human frailties, or so it seemed. It would also not be polite for him to do so. Letting the rookie know he could scarcely disagree was his weakness, if indeed the Guardian had any weaknesses. He shifted his weight, leaned more heavily on his spear, and allowed a mere hint of a smirk to show on his face. The sparkle in his eyes said it all, "We truly feel for you humans, but you never cease to amaze, and amuse us."

"Eight or nine wake-up calls..." Barnard began.

"Seven," came the swift reply.

"Seven it is," the mortal agreed. "You would know exactly. And I would never argue with the Boss."

"But you do," came the instant contradiction.

"Not now. Not any more. This is a whole new ball game, Bzutu. From now on I will do exactly what you tell me to do. That Satan worshipper at that cult place taught me a lesson. But with seven wake-up calls, I still have nothing to go on. Too often do I get it all wrong. But now I want to know exactly what gives."

Barnard watched the Warrior lean the spear against his shoulder. He had never seen him do that, never even seen him let go of that dangerous looking thing. Then, the Warrior's empty hands came up.

"Empty hands? You've got nothing? You mean to tell me you've got absolutely no idea what is going to happen?" Barnard asked.

"It is so," was ABC-22's answer.

Barnard had to think. "Don't go, please. Not yet. Let me think. Let me think." Eleven-eleven wake-up calls were coming in, but there was no information. That was a new one on George. "See if you can find out, Bzutu, please," he suggested. "I'll find you again tomorrow. Is that fine with you?"

"You all ways decide," was the answer. He was reminding Barnard of his human, not-negotiable free-will prerogatives.

"Yes, I all ways decide," the mortal agreed. "Ever since I met you, you've told me that on a score of occasions, my friend."

"More," came the instant response.

"Well. I have just now . . . all ways . . . decided that I will find you tomorrow," Barnard joked.

"We find you," the Spirit Guardian disagreed. Then he was gone. ABC-22 had made it clear that if he did not want to be found, he would never be found. His student might go and search for him, but it would always be the Guardian's locating George that put them in touch.

Barnard was terrorized by a frightening dream that warm and sultry night. None of his children could be found in their rooms. Their beds were empty, and the fear of them being lost woke him from his sleep. He urgently checked their rooms. They were all there! Fast asleep, and spread out on top of their blankets and in all kinds of directions. He tucked them neatly back under their sheets with a feeling of great relief, checked the deadlocks on the homestead's doors, just to make sure, then tried in vain to go back to sleep.

How do I really feel about leaving them behind, he wondered?

"Deeply troubled now. Damned miserable."

Gary Nixon was a lively, somewhat manic character. When bad judgement, worse luck, and abominable business circumstances threatened to put the Nixons out of their new home, Gary suffered a doozey of a nervous breakdown. That was bad timing. But Gary was resilient, took to hypnotherapy like a duck to water, and soon began to peg back his debts.

The Barnards had gotten to know his family—his wife Joyce, and their three children. They were the caring parents who would look after George and Jodi's offspring during the holidays. Westward bound, the Nixons would be returning to the town of their youth to stay on their parents' country properties.

"Gary and Joyce will be here on Sunday week," Jodi told her husband, "to discuss with us about the children. Clothes, toys, pocket money and all that, you know. And we should sort out how much we need to give them for living expenses for the kiddies."

"It's not going to happen," George told her bluntly.

"What do you mean?" she almost yelled at him.

"You will have only two children left when we get back," he answered.

The moment Jodi had spoken about Gary and Joyce Nixon turning up, Barnard knew their son would not be there on their return from Bali. There were no pictures to go with the knowledge. It was a cold, hard fact implanted in his mind—undeniable, inescapable, an absolute truth! And it made his blood run cold. The sudden knowledge of it had hit the Guardians' helper like a bolt out of the blue. Nothing else, in all those years, presented itself to his mind in such an abrupt, frightening fashion.

But Jodi wouldn't hear of it. "It's all arranged," she cried!

"It's all going to get unarranged," he told her gruffly. "Those three nippers are coming with us, Jodi."

"Talk to your Spirit Guides," she suggested. "Tell them to do something about it." Jodi was looking forward to the break. Her mind, once set in a certain mode, did not easily go for a re-think of any plan.

"Yes, I will, and, no, I don't," he told her. "Yes, I will talk with them. And no, I don't tell them what to do, ever. I'm only the lowest ranking critter in the platoon." He didn't tell Jodi she would lose her only son, but already Barnard was searching his very soul, and not finding any answers. Did he care more for the boy than he cared for his girls—Danielle and the little one? And if he did, how come he didn't know? It was wrong to love one child more than either or both of the other two. Plain stupid to love the boy more than the girls, he was telling himself. That can't be right!

"It'll take me hours to find the Guardians now," he told Jodi. "Christ! I'm stressed out of my mind over this thing."

"You look it," she agreed.

"Make sure I'm not disturbed in the clinic, please."

"I'll still wait for you," she answered. "You've got me worried, too. I've got to know, or I'll never sleep tonight."

She would likely be up for many hours, Barnard thought.

Laid back in his patients' recliner chair, the still deeply troubled George Mathieu drifted into the time realm of the Spirit Guardians with an ease he had not anticipated. Both, the Warrior and the androgynous Andréa were there. The vision was crystal clear.

It was hardly an achievement on Bzutu's part. He was a whiz at materializing, anywhere, and at any time. But, considering the time gap between the Androgynous One and the rookie, Andréa was performing brilliantly. She would be burning energy, and then some. Until that time, Barnard had only ever perceived her in profile, vaguely, distantly, if she cared to show herself.

The Androgynous One was the group's communicator, a messenger, and her motion picture thoughts were always in full color and had the depth of field of a hologram. Her vocal communication was a high-speed blurb of almost pure mathematics—Seraphim Talk—the language of the supernatural universe. Too fast to decipher for anyone of flesh and blood, only one's Spirit Self will perceive it. And if one's Spirit will not pass it on, it will elude the human mind every time.

Poor Andréa, he thought. She had long ago become the victim of George Mathieu's inhibitions, his ignorance and stupidity. In earlier years, the rookie had decided she performed no worthwhile function. The androgynous nature of the creature bothered him endlessly. And he suggested to her to get with it, move aside, or simply shove off altogether. That was ever so rude of him.

For some time, she refused to show herself, and then Barnard began to miss her. When she finally did turn up, she was always even more difficult to discern.

Not since that time, now quite some years ago, did he ever properly apologize for his rude behavior, although he always still greeted her quite cordially, seen or unseen. He generally sensed she was there. Not knowing whether she preferred to be a he, a she, or an it, he kind of christened her André-a. That still had not done it for him, and he promoted her to the status of an honorary female, and called her Andréa.

Force of habit made him turn to the majestic Warrior, but ABC-22 was scanning the horizon. He did not look up or reply. Only his mind, not his eyes, acknowledged the mortal's presence.

Then Andréa moved from her seat, and slowly, stiffly, turned to face her student. Their time-frame dissimilarities must have been the cause of her movement being so jerky. Momentarily, Barnard thought she might be ill with arthritis. She looked to be in agony. But that was sheer exertion making her pull a face like that.

This was the chance for him to finally apologize for his contemptuous behavior of the past. He was trying to formulate the sincere apology she rightfully deserved to receive. Too late! Her piercing eyes had transfixed him.

His thoughts were hampered. He could now only listen to her mind. Her time was limited, that was clear.

Generally, this ancient Guardian was hardly capable of transmitting her own image for any great length of time, let alone communicate at this ultra low level. Right there and then, she controlled his every thought.

"You are forgiven for two thousand years," was her mind-to-mind reply. She brushed aside his urgent need to be exonerated by her. Those were the eyes of a creature that knew only of love, compassion, and clemency. Here was the most brilliantly minded Guardian he had ever encountered.

"The children are involved, are they not, Andréa?" George asked. "You, also, love our children."

"All the children," she answered. She was including all people, all races, all ages. To Andréa all mortal races were her very own children.

"What will happen to our boy?" George asked.

Again, with a seemingly laborious effort, she showed Barnard the palms of her empty hands. Andréa simply did not know. She was there, doing Bzutu's job, and to indicate that even further up the chain of communication, things were still unknown.

Then she spoke, "Change your plans, or you surely lose the one you love."

What a beautiful voice! She had made a mighty effort to be heard. Functioning between Juliette's and ABC-22's time frames, the Androgynous One had been pushed to the limit to be heard. She was exhausted now, but she had gained great recognition from a desperately foolish mortal who had been so very discourteous.

"Grave danger," was the last mind-to-mind transmission.

The double meaning wasn't lost on Barnard. Grave as in serious, and grave as in burial, he concluded.

Andréa seemed to take ages to return to her seat. The effort of extending down to his timeframe had depleted the last of her energy.

"Thank you very much," George told her. Then he turned to the Warrior, but the Sentinel was still busily scanning the horizon, and he could tell George nothing more.

Sadly, Jodi was not prepared to accept the Spirit Guardians' advice. She hoped that somehow they would beat the odds. Plans were left in abeyance, but George Mathieu would simply refuse to depart on the appointed day, despite his having paid for the holiday in advance. He loved his kids, and trusted the Guardians with his, as well as the children's, lives. But Jodi had never seen a Spirit Guide, and perhaps she thought they and her husband could change anything, any time, anywhere.

The atmosphere in the homestead became far from amicable. The thought "Mexican standoff" frequently came to mind. George avoided open conflict, said nothing, did nothing to upset Jodi. He waited for more information, but he kept wondering if he really did care more for his boy, than he did for his two girls. Why would I? What has gone so desperately wrong with my upbringing, he wondered?

"You can't drag those kiddies all over the Philippines, Barnard," she complained.

"Three lazy weeks in Bali for all five of us," he told her, "doesn't sound so bad."

"It's all arranged!" she cried. "All the planes are booked . . . Buses . . . God!"

"It will all be unarranged, Jodi," he assured her, "with a little help from our celestial friends."

"It isn't like we've not been in Bali before," she muttered. "We climbed all over that island. And it was sizzling hot there!"

Barnard didn't have the stomach for an argument. He had nothing more to say.

Meditate on the concept of having been forgiven, centuries ago, for what you have not yet done wrong. If you can truly comprehend the wisdom contained in Andréa's message, you are going to suddenly find it awfully difficult to do anything at all wrong. But don't worry. You're human. You will keep making enough unintentional mistakes. And no one will be any the wiser about the sudden changes for the better in you.

2

A Child Under Glass

His vivid dream was the product of the highly experienced minds of the Seraphic twins he had
named Juliette—two great "Guys," but only one
name. After all, Barnard theorized, these two
shared everything else in life. And if they didn't like
each other by now, they would have long ago
parted company.

There had been so many of their lucid
dreams over the years, and George always enjoyed
them, especially in the knowledge that both deeply
caring Seraphim were nearby.

Although rarely perceived—and then more
often glimpsed by most fortunate patients, rather
than by the therapist—George Mathieu nearly
always sensed their presence.

He spoke with them, played the music they
enjoyed. And gradually, over the years, an
unashamed love affair developed between them.
"Them" . . . creatures of greatly differing origins
and destinies, but his ever-present Companions.

With their many thousands of years of experience, the Seraphim could generate an entire
range of pictures, colors, sounds, thoughts and
emotions. Although almost always unseen when in
the presence of the Spirit Guardians, they were
ever at hand. Now they were alone at the task of
bringing a vision of the future to the mortal's mind.
Soon, it would all become so intense he would

lose all realization of it being a lucid dream.

It would become ever so real—a gut-wrenching actuality.

It was a pleasant, carefree stroll on a crowded beach, with the sun beaming down on his back and shoulders. There was little wind, and a lazy surf. He knew this beach well.

At a distance, some forty or fifty people had formed a crowded circle at the water's edge. All were nearly motionless, shocked, silent, looking down at something that might have been deposited there by the waves. Already, George sensed that whatever it was that had so quickly caught their attention, it concerned him greatly, sadly, deeply. It would shatter his life into sorrowful fragments of inescapable suffering and endless self-blame.

He rushed towards this group.

With total disregard for the feelings of the many bystanders, he clawed his way to the center of the circle. There was the pale, seemingly lifeless body of a youngster. A child, not yet five years old. A boy he had given the name Michael. A cute, white-haired, blue-eyed little man, with a perpetual smile on his face. His only son.

There was no longer a smile on that little face.

He dropped to his knees in anguish, and reached out to touch him. He needed to know if the child was still warm, and if he was, then he might live. But he couldn't touch him.

Suspended in mid-air above this pale body was a large sheet of glass. On it the surf and the sand rolled back and forth and spilled from the side of the glass. He reached around the glass, but his child remained out of his reach. A life wasted for lack of care.

That smiling little fellow had not responded to urgent attempts at resuscitation by those who had found him.

Having awakened from a lucid dream, he was no longer certain of having seen the future or the past. Foolishly, he walked into the boy's room, and woke the little man from his sleep. Only when the child smiled at him, as he always did, did George fully realize it had all been a dream. With a hug, he tucked him back in. Seconds later, the boy was asleep again.

It was three o'clock in the morning. There was no chance of Barnard getting any more sleep that night. Aimlessly, he wandered around the house, brewing coffee, raiding the refrigerator, and acting more like a nervous patient than a cool therapist. Thinking, planning their vacation, arguing with Jodi in his mind, and wondering what he would be without the Guardians. *Bereaved, that's what I would be, and very soon.*

He made his way to the clinic, and boiled the jug for yet another coffee. He consulted his book of dreams, though he already knew. *The spilling of water from glass heralds the death of a child. He couldn't reach him, for he would be far away in the Philippines.*

It is flaming obvious! Why look it up in the book? Barnard! You fool! You knew all that! Stress . . . like never before.

But the Spirit Guardians had much more information now. Somehow, more detail had arrived since they last met. More than Danielle, more than the "baby," Michael had fretted about being left behind by his parents. He had wandered away from the party, and drowned in water little deeper than knee-high to an adult, and with so many people around! Someone had finally noticed him, but only just too late.

Belated efforts to revive the child had failed.

"Change your plans," Andréa repeated her clearly audible warning, "or you surely lose the one you love". She was not giving him the illusion of getting up again. Her previous stint of taking over Bzutu's job had drained her energy levels too much. Her reaching right down to his distant mortal mind was not really one of her regular pastimes.

Andréa always was the communications whiz, but not all the way down the line. Her chit-chat was with Beings even more distant than Seraphim. But the lingering uneasiness George had felt for so long with this androgynous Spirit Guardian had to be lessened somehow. It had been interfering with their performance as a platoon. This event, indeed, proved to be the turnaround. George finally realized that the Spirit Warrior was only his immediate contact in what might well be a very lengthy chain of command.

He was allowed to watch it all. Here was what one might call a signed and sealed Akashic record of the future, which was now going to be scrapped. This latest information, he was told, comes from far in time, and far in space. It was Paradise-generated information. ABC-22 made clear that the Spirit Guardians of the Halfway Realm had instigated negotiations for the release of the needed data.

As negotiations go, the Barnard family had been fiercely represented by them, and the Eleven-Eleven had stubbornly held out until they got just what they wanted, and not a crumb less. It was done.

The platoon's motto had always been, "We fight. We win. We all ways win." Barnard had heard it many times before, and it had nothing to do with pride. It stated a fact. The "fall-out" of this change to the mosaic of future events "reverberates around the globe many years," said ABC-22's mind.

Swiftly, the horror-in-the-making had been presented to the Seraphim, and they had volunteered to shock the living daylights out of their mortal.

Even though they knew George's new plans, Seraphim still never trust any of the fickle human minds. They cannot afford to trust people. Humans are renowned for changing their minds more often than their shorts.

For the mortal, it was an education, and then some.

He said, "Thank you all, you Guys," and took his mind back to the day Michael was born. George was there at his birth. "That baby arrived with a smile on his face," the attending nurse had commented with a laugh. Everyone had commented on it. Right from the start that smile had always been there, kind of saying, "Please love me."

For George, at that time, there had also been a most sinister feeling—a spine-chilling premonition that the cute little man would not be with the family for long. It had bothered him greatly, and for many months. Sudden Infant Death Syndrome is what the father had constantly feared.

This might well have been what long ago plagued my deeper conscious mind, he mused.

With just nine short days to go until their planned departure, there were now some major alterations to be made to that "mosaic of their time."

"Mr. Barnard, you are giving me an impossible task, because this is our busiest season. It's been booked out for months!" The helpful young woman sounded somewhat upset.

She might not know the Spirit Guardians are at work, George mused with a smile. "Yet today, you shall have the cancellations," he told her. Strike me pink, he thought! I don't talk like that! But I did say that. His fears had blown away. He was on an unbelievable high.

"Cosmic synchronization, kiddo," he told her. "My Friends and I have been busily fine-tuning the main gyro of this local universe, and for the last few weeks. We've got the entire galaxy running spot-on now," he joked. "It'll all be happening, and still today."

It was quiet on the other end of the line, and for quite some time. Then she said, "Your friend in business, who dropped in your proposed flight schedules, told me about you, and what you do. Yes, I believe it will all actually happen."

"That's the spirit!" he joked. "Go for it!"

He spent most of that Friday morning mediating between employees. The pre-Christmas holiday pressures were getting too much for some of his crew. Nothing fazed Barnard. By lunchtime, the travel agency was back on the line.

"Mr. Barnard," the young lady said in a disheartened voice, "will you believe me, if I tell you that what you have asked me to do just can't be done?" She told him what she had managed to do at that time, "I have cancelled all your flights and hotel accommodations. The works. But all I've got so far is you and your wife on a flight to Bali. No seats for the three children. There's no hotel space left on the island, and not a chance of procuring five seats on a flight to bring you all home. Honestly, it's hopeless!"

This young woman seems to be in urgent need of the services of a personal Spirit Assistant, he thought. "Just relax," he told her. "It's all going to happen, because I've already seen us on the other side. I've even peeked inside the hotel."

"What does the place look like?" she asked.

He told her precisely what it looked like, and she recognized it.

"I know that place!" She was delighted. "That's the Coconut Grove in Sanur!" she shouted. "I stayed there myself. I'll telephone them right away." She was on her way.

By ten minutes to five she was back on the line, saying, "This is your friendly travel agent reporting that the entire cosmos is now perfectly synchronized." She was getting into the spirit of things. It had all gone like clockwork.

There was, however, one problem, she told George. The Barnards would have to move into another hotel after the first two weeks. That was fine by George. The hotel will notify us, he thought. But somehow they all lost count of the days. And no one ever said anything. No one threw them out. They all stayed in the same rooms, for all of that time, and with a huge, friendly gecko for a pet.

George spoke to both Gary and Joyce Nixon. Neither of them sounded very pleased about his changing his plans. Although they understood he would miss the children too much, they also felt let down. They took it rather personally, George felt. The Barnards did not again meet up with them until about three months into the following year.

George did not intend to tell his wife about what he had done until the following day. She could first have a good night's sleep, and take all Saturday to heat up quickly, and cool down slowly, he felt. Frankly, the "hero" was also putting off what he thought might become a verbally violent confrontation. He hated that. No one ever wins an argument.

There would be no need to argue.

In the middle of the night, Jodi let out a scream. She managed to wake her husband faster then, than at any other time. She was sitting up in her bed, crying over a dream that would not go away. It was a fully-fledged night terror. It took ages for him to calm her down and make her realize it was only a dream. Finally, like he had done, she needed to check on the little man to see if he really was in his bed.

In the dream, she had found herself in a place in the mountains. She was describing Baguio City, and in great detail. A telegram had arrived to inform the Barnards they needed to immediately return home. Their boy was seriously ill. Then followed a long battle to get transport out of the place. And when they finally arrived back in the country, they rushed straight from the airport, to only just make it in time for their son's funeral.

A business friend living close by the Barnards, not the Nixons, had made the funeral arrangements. It sounded about right to George. The highly emotional Gary Nixon would have cracked up under the pressure of such trauma and resulting guilt. That was more than probable. Jodi's description of Baguio City was other than probable. It was dead-set accurate, though she had never been there. Brilliant!

Jodi Barnard, George suggests, was shown a part of what would have happened.

The entire episode left him wondering if he could ever repay the gallant Workers of the Halfway Realm. To this day, he thinks not. There had been other occasions when the quick-thinking Guardians averted George's being caught up in chaos on the roads. There were yet to be other incidents.

The rookie feels indebted to the Spirit Guardians, and much more so than the Guardians could possibly be indebted to him in well over thirty years of cooperation.

This time they saved the family from the devastating loss of a child. George is more than a little concerned about his own, at times, ineffective efforts.

Barnard's frequent feeble actions, pig-headed ideas, dumb pranks and hare-brained schemes of his many years as a mortal rookie in one of their platoons are all recorded, he's sure. It is but an insignificant chapter in the millennia-old chronicles of those of the Halfway Realm.

He shudders to think what the title of his small chapter might say:

GEORGE MATHIEU BARNARD
(A DOUBTFUL, COSTLY ACQUISITION)

The young Balinese man who chauffeured the family around the various sites on the island of Bali, was also a practicing hypnotherapist. That, of itself, was a bit of a fluke. Both he and George were developing some extensive visualization techniques. That was a lot more of a fluke. They shared a few valuable experiences and theories.

Barnard's Manila-based friend was not at home, George later learned. The healer was touring the US of A, lecturing and sightseeing. The Barnard couple would have arrived in front of a closed door.

The Baguio City contact was also missing, so George later found out from a mutual friend and colleague. It was his custom to travel throughout the provinces of the Philippines at that time of the year. Just as well the Barnards missed that place, too. It all started to look like "cosmic synchronization," whatever that could be.

But not until about the end of March, or early April, did they finally see the Nixon family again. What the Nixons related to them, brought home—no, it rammed home—to them was the frightening reality of the potential tragedy the Spirit Guardians had averted.

Joyce and Gary Nixon had also changed their holiday plans. They had not departed for their parents' inland cattle stations. Almost each day they had taken their three kiddies to the beach.

The very beach George knew so well.

Forever . . .

During the time it will take for these adventures
  to be documented, we promise
  that no animals will either be killed or injured in the
  production, by either the author or his immediate friends.

However, lots of people will lose their lives in wars,
  many will succumb to preventable diseases,
  and even more will lose the fight to hunger.

We obviously still keep forgetting
  we are collectively obliged to concern
  ourselves with the welfare of all . . .

and forever.

part two

The Eternity Conundrum

The Spirit Guardians of the temporal Halfway Realm had long ago greatly impressed George Mathieu with their honesty. At least the Warrior, ABC-22, touched Barnard with his businesslike attitude and directness. Not for a moment did the Guardian hesitate when questioned about his distant past. He readily admitted that "at a Time when there was no Law," his behavior had been somewhat unacceptable.

Barnard presumed that all ABC-22's regular Associates were of same or similar character. Again and again, they all proved to be reliable.

The mortal trusted his Teachers and Protectors. Since they turned up in his office, home, and clinic, talked sense, demonstrated a sense of humor and cared about others, they became an essential part of his life. He believed in them.

Far from spiritually "beautiful," Barnard believed in little else.

Yet, too many people who had never seen, touched, or spoken to a Spirit Guardian, professed to know what the universe and everything it contained was all about. The majority disagreed with each other about essential details and most of them argued. A few learned to hate George Mathieu Barnard, whose association with the Guardians was seen by them as his being in alliance with the supposedly ever-present Satan himself.

Some acquaintances even became violent.

It could well have been that if Barnard had acquired strong fundamentalist religionist leanings, he would have instantly rebuffed the Spirit Guardians' advances. Despite his many faults, that discerning open-mindedness might well have been what was needed to make the mortal their potential aide and student.

The Guardians had severely shaken George's world with that view of the future that "comes from far in time, and far in space." The Androgynous Guide had spoken about a horrific, already existing, but still vague reality. On learning the details, the Seraphim swiftly produced the pictures and feelings of a "now-time" tragedy. And finally, ABC-22 had explained about the origin of the data, in easy-to-grasp detail.

None of the group had so far chosen to communicate in a past or future tense. As always, it was all happening "now." Their concept of the passing of time had always been different from how Barnard saw it. He felt sure they were telling him that the records had come from Eternity—a place where all time/space events are "pooled," or simply pre-known and understood. Perhaps events were released just a little at a time, to make reality possible for the demands for temporal continuity in the time/space worlds.

Since childhood he himself had many visions of events of the future. But he was never so bold as to call his remarks about future events prophecy. His psychology lecturer, Professor Edward Willis claimed it really was, and that Barnard's Spirit Self alone could bridge the gap between all-knowing Eternity and mortal "linear" time. Spirit Guardians were only used to bounce ideas off.

That assumption had now been proved to be false.

But with an inborn uneasiness about the origin of his childhood premonitions, Barnard had avoided giving both prophecy and Eternity much thought. An old Indian Guru had also alarmed eighteen-year-old George Mathieu with his predictions about the young man's future. Perhaps, at that time, Barnard only unsettled himself even more. He simply did not want to be that kind of a freak.

For many years after meeting the Guru, George avoided postulating about the anatomy of both prophecy and Eternity. Theories of multi-dimensional time always intrigued him more.

Now he had more thinking to do. Time and perhaps even motion, but Eternity and prophecy, obviously, all interplayed in the psychic events that were an ongoing part of his bizarre life.

3

Swami Sarasvati

It was a chance meeting in Australia that brought the barely eighteen-year-old Dutch migrant into contact with the Guru, Swami Sarasvati. Year after year, more of the Indian psychic's predictions about the strange life Barnard would lead came true.

There was no denying this fact.

At the time of their meeting, Sarasvati had at first astounded the young man with the accuracy of his knowledge of Barnard's past. Soon after, George Mathieu felt somewhat overawed by the massive amount of personal information about his life this total stranger seemed to have. Finally, Barnard became alarmed, shocked into disbelief, quite frightened and almost paralyzed on the spot, by what the Hindu teacher saw in his future. In the end, Barnard walked out on the Guru, spooked, upset, determined to give the man a wide berth if he ever saw him again.

They would never meet again, at least not face-to-face. But in the years that followed, George Mathieu would often regret his having retreated in fear and with great haste from that rather opportune encounter.

Most of Barnard's co-workers used to get together for a cold beer on Fridays after work. Friday was the firm's payday, and being paid for another week of hard work was considered to be an excellent reason for a short celebration at the corner pub.

It had taken his colleagues a few tries to convince their work mate, new from Europe, that the arctic-cold Australian beer was the best in the world. It alone was seen as sufficient reason for anyone to migrate to the Land Down Under. It was even claimed the mere smell of that precious drop of amber fluid was enough for hordes of foreigners to come and stay.

George Mathieu, except for the Fridays on which he was sent out on a message for his firm, frequently joined up with the tribe for a well-deserved beer and a game of darts.

One particular Friday, a stranger was seated quite alone at their usual table near the dartboard. Pakistani, or Indian, Barnard thought. The man was very dark, short, and grossly overweight, with a big round head and unusually long hair. He smiled an almost toothless smile at the group and gestured for them all to take up their regular table. Remarkably, he in some way already seemed to know it was their usual table.

Robert, the second eldest, and easily the most outgoing of Barnard's colleagues, reached across the table and shook hands with the stranger. "Rob McArdie," said Robert, "good to meet you."

"Sarasvati," answered the man with hardly a trace of an accent. "Swami Sarasvati. And I see you have a most energetic wife and four children." That could hardly have been a guess. Robert McArdie did have four youngsters. And Robert McArdie did, certainly, have a most unstoppable wife. Jan McArdie was involved in all kinds of social activities.

This strange and overweight, sharp-eyed but somewhat neglected-looking man had a mind power that was fast and accurate. Or did he? Barnard himself, albeit infrequently, was in the habit of making the most unlikely assertions that, somehow—only God knows how—turned out to be embarrassingly accurate.

Sarasvati's remarks elicited a loud and nervous giggle from little Donna, the youngest member of the group, who was only allowed to join her workmates if she stuck with her lemon squash. But the teenager, with lights in her eyes and a big expectant smile on her face, bravely stepped forward in turn to shake hands with a man who seemed to know things that could simply not be known. "I'm Donna," she said with a tense laugh.

"And you are almost out of your apprenticeship and about to set up house with the love of your life," Sarasvati answered. That was another "bull's eye." Right on the mark that was. Donna had many brothers and sisters and had also recently been given her parents' permission to go it alone once she received higher wages.

Barnard was intrigued by it all, but distrustful. Perhaps everyone here already knows this Sarasvati fellow, he thought. And, perhaps, Sarasvati knew all of them before I became a regular visitor to our corner pub. Suddenly he realized that he, too, tended to turn up unexpectedly in places where he had never meant to go, only to occasionally find his presence to be enigmatically opportune, even appropriate.

"My name is Ethel," said Mrs. Deane, the company's head of quality control, and the eldest of the group. She seated herself between Robert and Donna and put out her slender hand with the many bejeweled rings it sported. "I like that name, Sarasvati, you chose for yourself."

"I like the effort your son is putting into his studies," Sarasvati replied. "He will be an eminent surgeon in his field." Ethel's only son, Jason, was studying medicine somewhere. Barnard did not know where Jason was studying. But the supposedly clever young man had made a worrying, painfully slow start and only in recent months suddenly improved his marks out of sight.

Something was happening here that George Mathieu did not understand. He was the only one still on his feet and about to turn for the bar to get all of them, including Sarasvati, a drink. "Shake hands with George," Ethel suggested to Sarasvati, "and tell me what I already know." It sounded like a challenge of some kind.

"I'm getting the drinks," said Barnard. He was uneasy.

"No. I'm getting them," said Robert McArdie. "A beer?" he asked Sarasvati, and since the Swami nodded, Robert left for the bar saying, "I know what you're all having."

Rather gingerly, George Mathieu approached the Indian man and held out his hand. It was a warm handshake.

"You have healing hands," Sarasvati remarked. "Very much so." That was the second time Barnard had heard that ridiculous remark. It was in fact Ethel Deane who had told him that just a few days earlier during a coffee break.

"Didn't I tell you?" she asked George Mathieu. "Be honest now. Didn't I tell you?"

"You did say that," Barnard admitted. But he was suspicious now. Sarasvati's presence seemed like a set-up

Barnard had been lured into. A trick. And just the kind of practical joke Robert McArdie was famous for organizing.

Momentarily, Sarasvati appeared to be deep in thought. Then he said, "You chose to be a healer instead of a warrior, and you came all this way for the purpose." He looked Barnard in the eyes, and the young man knew Sarasvati had it right. The man was truly perceptive, and far beyond the normal, for no one in the firm had ever been told Barnard was a conscientious objector.

Soon their round of drinks arrived, and the conversation shifted to the mundane as everyone took part in a few games of darts. But as the others were about to go home, the Indian Guru addressed George Mathieu. "Stay for a moment longer," he suggested. "There is so much you need to know."

Still rather in two minds about Sarasvati's offer, Barnard told his colleagues he'd see them the following Monday, returned to his table, and prepared himself for more fortune telling adventures from this unusual man.

"Why did you not want to become a soldier?" Sarasvati asked.

Barnard sighed. "It was strange," he finally admitted. "I don't really believe in reincarnation of the soul. I do feel that one's Spirit Self may have previous experiences, but I don't waste much time thinking about it. There are vague, but very real and kind of sad memories in my mind of my having wielded a deadly sword. Too much killing. Too many dead. And then, I was called up to become a hussar, you know, a Queen's Guard. It brought my studies to a sudden end. Not that I was doing extra well at the time. More interested in girls. I was kinda lost, anyway. And that was bad enough, but there were some uneasy feelings about entering the armed forces."

"You saw yourself injured," Sarasvati suggested.

Barnard raised his eyebrows at the Guru in disbelief. He was left speechless for the moment.

"You *did* see yourself injured," Sarasvati maintained. He was stating a fact. "Seriously injured, and in a routine training exercise."

"Yeah," Barnard admitted at last, "you're right. You're only too right. But I don't know precisely how or when I would have got hurt. There were to be plenty of opportunities. Hopping out of an airplane in the middle of the night from, the Lord knows, way up there. Driving a three-meter high tank through a four-meter deep canal. Garroting some poor guy with a piano wire on two sticks in a trench during the dim, dark hours. But what bothered me most was the idea the training would destroy my mind, make me ruthless. It was actually quite an honor for my folks to have a family member in the Queen's very own guards. It broke their hearts when I decided that it was not for me. I was told I had two options: Join the Guards, or spend two years in prison. I thought of the third option all by myself, and got the devil out of there, pronto. It had always been my idea to migrate to Australia. I hadn't planned to leave in such a hurry."

Barnard hesitated. "That's not strictly true, actually. It would be fairer to say I always knew I would leave the country and go far away to Australia. And I didn't so much know it. I saw it. Strange, isn't it? I was only five or six."

Sarasvati nodded. "You saw it right and you did it right," he suggested. "You would have been very badly hurt. There's much for you to do in this life. You will start a business, too. And healing others, you know. You have great, great, extrasensory abilities, you know that."

He had made George Mathieu laugh with that serious look on his big, round face. "You're not doing too bloody bad yourself, Swami," the young man's answer came. "I'm sorry. That was factory talk. A bit rude." Barnard was feeling nervous. The guru was making him feel as if he were naked.

But with an impatient wave, Sarasvati ostensibly dusted Barnard's apology from the table. He was becoming animated in his speech as he told George Mathieu of Jehanne Colette, Barnard's older, and only, sister, who was commonly referred to as Jéjé. He almost got her name right, and he certainly knew how close she and George had been. There was George's older brother, who never let up in telling his younger sibling what an extraordinary fool and dreamer of a kid he was.

He was sounding even more inspired now as he described George's mother, her psychic instincts and abilities. Much more of an accent was slowly sneaking into Sarasvati's words as he outlined George's father's apprehension about all things psychic. He knew George had five brothers, one of whom had died rather young.

This is getting too damned creepy for me, Barnard was telling himself. He wanted out of that pub, onto his train, and into a decent meal at his boarding house.

Suddenly the Indian man fell silent. He seemed to be deep in thought, but only for a few seconds. "What's the date of your birth?" he asked sharply. "Oh, and where were you born?" And as George told him, he penned it down on a beer coaster. "Aha," he said, busily drawing grids, numbers, and connecting lines. "Aha, aha, aha . . . Aha!" He seemed to have found something worthwhile. "What time? What time? What time?" he wanted to know.

"Just on half past eleven at night," Barnard answered. He felt pleased he at least knew something most people did not.

"You will be surrounded by many Spirits," Sarasvati told him at last. "You already are! Even now! Lucky! So fortunate!" The man was getting more excited by the moment. Barnard was getting more bothered, self-conscious. He was beginning to blush, and he knew it. Darn! Not again. Many of the regulars in the hotel were staring at the two men near the dartboard. Embarrassing!

"I have to go home now, Mr. Swami," George Mathieu told him.

"Sit there!" Sarasvati ordered. "Sit there and listen. This is important."

"I really . . ." Barnard tried again.

"You stay," Sarasvati commanded. "You will receive great dispensations. You will come face to face with Avatars. You will know so many Spirits. You will be baptized again by the Creator's fire and be re-born, and you know nothing now. I have to tell you about these things." He sounded kind of angry, aggravated.

Possessed by something evil, Barnard mused like the good little Christian boy he tried to be?

George Mathieu stood and turned on the loudly objecting Guru. "I have to tell you something, too! Right now, Mr. Swami! I don't even know one Avatar, and I don't want to end up in a burning house, or something. And I was baptized a long time ago with a dash of holy water, and that'll do me for keeps."

"Please? Please?" the man answered. He seemed to suddenly realize Barnard was fearful of him. "If you must really go, take my card. Come and see me when you feel better. I will teach you many things you must know. For many hours I will teach you, and not charge you one penny. Please? You must learn of the Golden Fire."

"Okay," Barnard told him, and took the card. He left, thoroughly overwhelmed and utterly spooked by Sarasvati's agitated behavior.

"Phew!" he expressed when safely out of the hotel. "How many like him, are wandering around outside their cages in the great land of the Ganges?"

Finding out that Swami simply means Mr. or Teacher, or something, that Sarasvati was really the name of a Goddess, and Avatars were thought to be reincarnated Gods, helped Barnard to soon shrug off the unusual experience. It was much harder to forget Swami Sarasvati's big round face and urgent dental needs.

In later years, as George Mathieu felt himself caught-up in an ever-growing "avalanche" of psychic experiences, he came to regret not having stayed with Sarasvati. Even more did he bemoan not having returned to visit the Guru at his home before the man returned to his native land.

At the time, the Indian wise man had most unwisely scared the young migrant out of his eighteen-year-old wits. Undoubtedly, Sarasvati, or whoever he really was, had recognized psychic or spiritual potential in the young man. He had also wrongly presumed this same young man to be as excited about that as he himself was.

That was hardly the case. Not then.

When Human Free Will "Dissolves"

The pendulum swings.
Civilizations rise.
Then they crumble and fall.
War and diseases may decimate us.

A ten-year view can be disturbing.
A century may seem chaotic.
But over many millennia there is steady evolutionary
    progress.

Left to our own inclinations,
    and our essential human free will franchises,
    our world would slowly and inevitably go into decline.

But every once in a while,
    the valiant Guardians of the Halfway Realm,
    Those they serve, and those who may serve them,
    are permitted to coerce the natural flow of events,
    without fuss, and
    for a better outcome, when

Human Free Will must be "Dissolved."

part three

Serving the Guardians

In his spare-time involvement as a clinical hypnotherapist, Barnard had a bit of an "attitude." Whereas his highly profitable business enterprise brought him financial security, his clinic provided him with only scant monetary rewards. Frequently, the therapist would not even charge his regular fee. Often, if his patient was having a difficult time, he would never even send her, or him, a bill.

"The business is sucking the lifeblood out of the community," he used to say. "The clinic spits it back in. The end result is progress all around. Who cares about the money?"

Barnard well knew he was respected, and very successful as a practicing therapist. He was intuitive in gauging his patients' needs, resourceful, but he would be altogether useless as a full time therapist. He knew he would surely not last a year in that capacity.

Being too sensitive, too emotional, and his getting personally involved, were serious handi-caps he learned to live with. Enough was enough of an endless flow of human misery, and he would then escape to his factory to solve technical problems. Variety of involvement stimulated his ever-searching mind.

His attitude did not stop there, either. Overweight patients should stop eating so much, he felt. Those with mild phobias should learn to live with it. Nicotine addicts should throw away their smokes, if they were fed-up with the habit. And if they weren't, Barnard would likely offer them one of his own cigarettes.

Most general inquiries were passed onto a friend, a clinical psychologist, who had her cozy, classy little clinic not far from the Barnards' home.

His unprofessional bent for refusing to treat so many common cases still left Barnard with an ample supply of patients to treat in the limited time he could contribute to the cause. Moreover, there were other forces at work.

Many of his patients were clearly guided to his clinic door by the Spirit Guardians of the Halfway Realm. And most of these were desperate people, deeply troubled or badly mistreated, often suicidal.

"Where do you get all these people?" his psychologist friend once asked on a visit to the Barnard clinic. "Each and every one of these cases constitutes major mischief!" She sounded exasperated. "George, honestly, I have great respect for you, but you are not yet anywhere near adequately qualified to handle the majority of these conditions."

"I know. I know. But they're all referrals, Veronah," Barnard answered.

"Who is irresponsible enough to send them to you?" she demanded to know.

"My Spirit Guardians," he told her quietly, "but they're good enough to stick around and help me with the treatments."

Veronah Miller gave him a long, hard look. Then came a deep sigh.

"You and your Spirits . . ."

4

Stephen Laurence

Clinical Psychologist Veronah Miller often considered her many time-consuming hypnotic procedures to be the superior method of treatment. Veronah preferred to spend extra time with some of her patients in the knowledge that hypnotherapy tended to produce more powerful and lasting, positive new habit patterns compared to ordinary counseling. Undoubtedly, her distinct accent was a significant aspect of what so securely established new or modified behavior in her clients' daily lives.

The tall, only "slightly aging" Lithuanian-born blonde conducted her busy practice just a few kilometers down the road from Barnard's clinic. She, like George Mathieu, had once been one of Professor Willis' students. Miller and Barnard frequently exchanged specific information, often sought one another's opinions on cases, and they both belonged to the same hypnosis society. At the conclusion of the society's periodic evening meetings, the psychologist and the therapist usually met for a drink and a talk on some deep subject about which they would endlessly argue and rarely agree.

They had become unlikely though mutually respectful friends.

Veronah, according to Barnard, was all painstaking logic and endless tiresome reasoning. She was meticulous, a left-brain specialist, and she never appeared to forget anything she learned. That, undoubtedly, was Veronah's strength. But she would probably never invent anything new, even develop any kind of theory of her own. To Veronah the universe was an accident, the human mind the ultimate last dimension, and God, if He or She ever lived, had long ago left the place in disgust.

Barnard, according to Mrs. Miller's frequently voiced opinion, relied not on facts, but on an over-active imagination, which he allowed to masquerade as intuition. Sheer hard work is what made him successful, in both business and clinical work. And if he ever outgrew his "childhood fantasy" Spirit Guardians and began to more seriously employ any part of his brain, left or right, he would be even more successful. He should clear his head of the wild theories it contained before they sent him permanently around the twist.

So argued Veronah.

A young man with long blond hair accompanied Veronah. George had not seen him before at any of the meetings. Veronah waited until they arrived at a free table, drinks in hand, before doing the introductions. "George, this is Stephen Laurence," she said. "Stephen, meet George Barnard."

"Pleasure meeting you, George," drawled Stephen as he put down his drink and shook Barnard's hand. He sounded very American.

"Good to see you, Stephen," Barnard told him, vaguely wondering how he could know so much about this young fellow whom he had never met before. "What's a twenty-two-year-old from California doing in the Land Down Under, Stephen?" he asked. "And did your mother back in LA agree to let you travel all by yourself?" The therapist tried hard to smile as he spoke those rather condescending words. Finally he also realized he was wide awake and doing what normally he could only do in a trance.

This was the very same thing Swami Sarasvati had done to him so long ago, with equal ease, in similar surroundings, and with similar results. Stephen was looking a bit bewildered, even a little fearful.

For a moment there was no reply to Barnard's tongue-in-cheek remark, but Stephen quickly glanced at Veronah who was shaking her head. Then he said, "Jesus, you're sharp."

"Jesus was much sharper, Stephen," Barnard laughed. "Now, He was *sharp,* that Man!"

The young American, still in doubt, looked at Veronah again and there were questions on his face, like, "How could he know?" and, "You must have told him." But there was not a sound from the young American.

Veronah shook her head again, clearly denying she had said anything, then she turned to Barnard. "Stephen is staying with Hal Miller and me," she explained. The psychologist avoided inventing an explanation for what Barnard had just perceived and expressed about Stephen Laurence. She, too, tended to be a little spooked by Barnard's picking people's brains when it occasionally happened. And as always, she referred to her husband as Hal Miller, not Harold, or my husband.

"We've got Stephen for eight days, George, that's all. Then he's got to go bush, for a film-shoot. A wildlife documentary. Stephen is my nephew, my sister's only son, and we haven't seen him for four years, five almost." She carried on with a smile, "I did tell him you pick people's brains, but that you believe you employ a platoon of Spirit Guardians when you should really give some credit to your own dizzy little mind."

Veronah did not believe in Spirit Guardians. Everything Barnard learned from their realm, in her view, happened within Barnard's own mind. She enjoyed having a dig at the therapist about the Guardians and how they worked hard without ever appearing on his payroll or demanding money under the table.

"I have friends back in LA who have Spirit Guides," Stephen offered.

Barnard nodded. "Lots of people have, Stephen," he assured the young man. "But the Spirit Guardians I know have me. They are a special group without names. They have only alphabetical/numerical codes." He poked out his tongue at Veronah. "They gave me a glimpse of your sister, Mrs. Miller, and she doesn't look a bit like you. She's shortish and she's got short dark hair, maybe black."

Stephen Laurence looked intrigued. "You've got that right," he assured Barnard. "You're beginning to blow my mind! Are you going to come with us and do some more of that tonight?"

"Hal Miller asked me to invite you," Veronah confessed. "He's made a huge batch of potato wine and he wants you to help him drink some of it." She added, "It's beautiful, George. Best batch he's ever made."

"It's almost nine o'clock," Barnard remarked. He still had some therapies to write that evening and he wasn't

sure if he cared for Harold Miller's wine. He liked potatoes, but fried, boiled, as chips, even mashed.

"Doing what you call "some more of that" doesn't
always work, Stephen," he suggested. Perhaps it will, he
thought. Perhaps it is time for this young man to learn
something new. But as he followed Veronah and Stephen
in their car to the Millers' home, he wondered if he would
be wasting his time, and he considered how much more
he himself could have learned from the guru, Swami
Sarasvati, than he could possibly teach Stephen Laurence.

Harold Miller, a self-employed surveyor, had always
been a soft-spoken man. In fact, he hardly ever spoke.
And perhaps surveyors tend to point, wave, and give all
kinds of strange signals out in the field. Perhaps this
became a habit over the years. His wife surely made up
for his silence, professionally, one might suggest. But on
this evening Hal loudly bemoaned the loss of his treasured red wine, due to an "aggressive bug." The Shiraz was
spoilt, sour and useless. He praised his potato wine for
many minutes. He was right. It was brilliant, and they all
enjoyed it, as well as the company. It was getting very
late. They had talked for hours. Barnard needed to get
started if he was going to try to entertain Stephen.

Like George Mathieu, Stephen had seated himself on
the floor. He could hardly wait for the therapist to pick up
on his mother again. Just moments after Barnard dropped
into a trance, he found himself in someone's home. The
session would quickly become one of the most colorful
"overseas visits" he ever attempted.

"Got your mom," he told Stephen. "She doesn't understand you very well, does she?"

"They all want me to work in the business," he admitted, "and I hate it."

The short, dark-haired woman was standing in the middle of the room, lost in thought, oblivious to Barnard's presence. Quite overweight, she checked out to be healthy all the same. "Such a placid natured woman." He was drawn to her kitchen. "Two steps down and you're in her kitchen," he said. "It's huge! She must love this kitchen."

"She's a really good cook," Veronah chimed in, "even when she was little."

Barnard looked around her kitchen and described what he saw. "The cupboards are a blond timber, and the tops are olive green. There are two, four, five copper pots with black handles hanging on the wall above the stove. Ah, you can't cook with them! They're just decoration. There is a row of tiles that goes all around. Let me see. It's a horn of plenty design in stacks of colors. There's a lot of light here with the sunshine beaming in."

"It's early morning over in the States, George," Stephen suggested.

"Oh, yes," Barnard said. It would take too long for him to explain to Stephen that he could look at yesterday during tomorrow and see next week on the Sunday just past. But nearly all the bright scenes he had witnessed in the past were kind of dull compared to this. This looked like it was floodlit. "Time means little," Barnard mumbled.

"Time for another glass of wine," Veronah suggested and Barnard popped back up from the trance.

"It's a really beautiful home. And it's big," Barnard remarked.

"Is my guitar still on my bed?" Stephen asked.

Everyone laughed at his comment. "If it isn't, I didn't steal it just then. And I didn't look." Barnard replied. "But what I just saw was in bright color and I sometimes get only shades of gray and bits of color."

"It's the potato wine," Hal suggested softly. He was pouring another glass for everyone. "It goes with everything and everything goes with it. Have some more and whiz back again." He was unsteady on his feet. "Drink up. This will get you there twice as fast."

Barnard checked the time. It was well after midnight. "I hate it when people throw me out of their homes," he suggested.

"No, no, no," Veronah chimed in. "You're doing well. I'll show you my pictures of the place, after. You're doing good. Go on."

Coming from her, that sounds odd, Barnard thought. She can be so critical, so consistently. This is all for Stephen's benefit.

"Do your Spirit Guides take you there?" Stephen wanted to know.

Barnard shrugged. "Probably. Who knows? But it works, mostly."

Ten minutes later, he was back in LA, moving around outside Stephen's house and feeling deeply frustrated. Whichever way he tried, he could not get into the place. Someone was interfering with his free will to move about. The doors were locked, the windows were shut. "I can't get inside now," he complained.

"Try the back door," Stephen suggested. "It's always open."

"Not now," George told him. "Here's something on four legs," he joked. "It's little. White, black and a bit of brown. Three guesses."

"That's Chippie!" Stephen sounded excited. "You found my trusty hound."

Barnard was beginning to feel impatient. He tried the door once more, but it wouldn't budge. Moving around the yard, he felt drawn to the front of the home. Finally, he wandered into the wide suburban street, disgusted with his own efforts, suspicious of his being controlled. His free will prerogatives had been dissolved.

There was a young girl in tennis costume coming towards him. She was carrying an old airways bag on her right shoulder. With her tennis racket in her right hand, she lovingly trailed her left hand over the untrimmed shoots of a privet hedge. There was something beautiful, energetic and arresting about this otherwise rather plain, rather plump young lady with hair down to her waist.

"Did you leave a girlfriend behind, Stephen?" Barnard asked.

"No," He answered. He muttered something about being engaged to the film industry.

"What a beautiful person," Barnard said. He described her as he kept pace with her.

"Could it be . . . No," Stephen said. "Not her."

"She has used her hair to tie up her hair," Barnard remarked. "Pretty clever. Two long locks from the side and she has tied them into a bow. Wait on! Wait on!"

The girl had just turned onto the path to Stephen's house, pushed a key into the lock and stepped inside. With only inches to spare, Barnard slipped in behind her. Soon, he witnessed an animated conversation between the young lady and Stephen's mother. There was little he could understand. It all came much too fast for him, but he did comprehend the gist of what was being discussed. He surfaced from the trance.

"That was BJ you were talking about," Stephen remarked.

Barnard yawned and reached for his potato wine. "She's quite lovely," he said. "Who is she and what did you call her just then?"

"BJ! She's my kid sister. BJ. Belinda Jane. She ties her hair like that all the time. And there's nothing lovely about her," Stephen muttered. He got up from the floor and looked down on Barnard with a smirk on his face. "BJ is BJ. BJ is a dawg."

"A what?" That crude remark had made George angry. He had been so impressed with the young lady, so quickly. Momentarily, he had shared the strength, the optimism, the vivacity that glowed all around her. "Her mind!" George shouted at Stephen. "Personality, drive, soul, spirit, essence, Mister. Assets you'll never acquire in your life. Who cares about bodies?" He had said it, and quickly realized there was no way he could unsay those things. Better blame the potato wine, he thought.

"Give it a break, you two," Veronah suggested sharply.

"Plain Jane, Belinda Jane," Stephen Laurence muttered. "The kid's a pest, a dumb little squirt."

"You grew up with one of the most caring young ladies I ever looked at in this crappy world," George told him. He agreed the girl was far from beautiful, but she had charm, and then some. "Find yourself a good looking body without a soul," he suggested angrily. "That's what you deserve and should be on the lookout for. But you'll never know how privileged you were to have her for a sister. Anyway, the squirt's getting married. Bloody good riddance to brother Stephen, I'd say."

Veronah was the quickest to respond. "What are you saying?"

"She's getting married," Barnard repeated. "Like having a wedding. People do that kind of thing, I don't know . . . practically all over the world, they say. And I think I should be going home now."

"She's nineteen!" Stephen Laurence shouted at him in anger.

Barnard had to think about what he had said. "Yeah? Really? She looks even younger, I think."

"You've got a bloody screw loose!" He was shouting at Barnard.

"So, why are *you* coming undone? You're the one who's coming unglued, Son," Barnard fired back at him. "Give *me* that break." He turned to Veronah. "I can't handle this senseless aggravation. It was a big mistake coming here tonight. Teach the kid some relaxation in the morning. Better still, zap him out and forget to wake him up for a few days. It might not be too late for one short-fused Yank." He tried to find his feet.

It wasn't easy, for Stephen Laurence wasn't giving in so quickly. He was blocking Barnard's way, crowding him. He needed to convince George he'd got it all wrong, or convince himself it was wrong. There was fear in his eyes and for the first time Barnard realized he might be frightened of losing his sister. Stephen Laurence loved that stubby little "squirt" after all, and, perhaps, he had only just realized he did love her. Maybe he was just abrupt by nature.

"She isn't even engaged!" he shouted. He sounded desperate.

Barnard had now begun to doubt what he had seen, and doubt what he had heard and picked-up on intuitively. People do get engaged first, and then they plan their weddings, he thought. "I calls it as I sees it," he answered defensively. "I don't make it happen. And maybe I got it wrong. Who knows?"

The telephone rang and Veronah reached for the headset.

"Have some more potato wine," said Hal Miller. He was already filling Barnard's glass. "Saved by the bell," he whispered. "Nothing exciting ever happens in our home, but tonight's just great."

"It's for you, Steve," said Veronah. "It's your mom."

The young man darted for the telephone.

This could be the right time for this hypnotherapist to make himself scarce, Barnard thought. However, he had been sitting on the floor for too long. His legs had now gone numb and he was struggling to get up. He surrendered for the moment and sipped some more potato wine.

Stephen wasn't saying much, except, "Oh," and again, "Oh." Then they all heard him loudly say: "It's already ages past midnight here. I remember that guy from College, Mom." The young American was touching his pockets, feeling for his cigarettes. He was nervously looking around the room for an ashtray, perhaps, or for a reaction from all those present. A war would break out if he accidentally lit up and smoked in the Millers' sacred domain.

Veronah was pricking up her ears. She reached out to Barnard, tightly squeezed his arm and wouldn't let go of it. Hal, it appeared, had stopped breathing entirely. Of all those present, George Mathieu was the very last to catch on.

"But we already know, Mom. Hold on, Mom. Hold on." Stephen held the telephone away from his face and vaguely smiled at everyone. "BJ's gettin' hitched," he said. It was clear to all he was scarcely aware of what he was saying.

"Yes! Yes! Yes!" shouted Veronah. She was now hurting George's arm in a vice-like grip.

Hal had found another bottle and was topping up the glasses one more time, mumbling, "A celebration."

"There's a man here and he flies around and looks at people," Stephen explained. "No, not a fortune-teller."

"A bit like Mary Poppins," Hal suggested. He looked all done in, a bit unsteady, but his ready wit had remained unaffected, if the wine hadn't improved it.

He would be late at work the following morning, George thought. Seating himself on the floor now, with two more bottles of potato wine by his side, Hal Miller might be camping out on his living room floor for days to come. Barnard felt it was wrong for them all to be listening to Stephen's conversation, but no one else was getting up. Barnard, too, was enjoying himself, guessing what was being said at the other end.

"No, he's not a spy. He's a friend of Auntie Vee's and Uncle Hal's. He saw you and BJ and Chippie. And he likes the house and the kitchen." It sounded so pathetic.

Hal Miller was cracking up with laughter and Veronah, tears running down her cheeks, finally let go of George's arm.

Barnard left almost unnoticed. There was a crate with a dozen bottles of potato wine on the front seat of his car.

That was so typical of the thoughtful Harold Miller.

"One day . . . One day one of you might turn up in Veronah's clinic and speak to her directly," Barnard suggested to the Spirit Guardians. "I'm getting fed up with you Guys not being accepted by her."

Barnard still questions: Who or what stopped me from entering Stephen's home during that second attempt? Why so much detail in such bright colors? And what about the timing? The telephone call from Stephen's mom so shortly after the session explained everything Stephen needed to know. Surely there was no great need for Barnard to do what he did when he did it.

Perhaps Harold Miller, or Veronah, at last, had something to learn. But the regular arguments with Mrs. Miller continued, and Hal never mentioned the episode again. The psychologist stuck with her conviction that nothing other than Barnard's highly imaginative mind had "fluked" the entire thing.

It was difficult to escape the notion that all three had been intrigued by it, as well as a little fearful of it, not unlike Barnard had reacted to Sarasvati's visions and predictions.

But perhaps Stephen Laurence did have something to learn, and this was the preferred way. Perhaps the young man needed to realize he did care for his sister, that there was more to living than wildlife documentaries. Perhaps it had been time for him to develop a greater spiritual or psychic awareness.

5

José Goldblum

It used to be called Shell Shock. Later it was defined as Battle Fatigue. It now goes by the name of Post-Traumatic Stress Disorder. You may casually call it PTSD if you are exchanging information with a colleague, or if you want to vainly impress others with your extraordinary knowledge of psychology.

One and the same disorder, it will probably get yet a few more names in years to come. Teased apart into subgroups, for which all kinds of clever, professional-sounding names may yet be invented, it will probably always be hard to treat and frequently fail to respond to treatment. The healing process can take many years and, at times, the patient may never fully recover.

It is not limited to soldiers at the front lines. Seemingly, everyone is a candidate. A violent assault, a particularly nasty home invasion, an armed hold-up, and even a severe natural disaster, illness or accident can produce a flourishing PTSD.

In the case of José Goldblum, a victim of inhumanity perpetrated by "sub-humans" on a most undeserving guy, the abrupt effects of this newly acquired mental disorder were nothing less than astounding in their ferocity. This out-going, resourceful, optimistic and boisterous pillar of the local Latin Community was suddenly reduced to a fearful, quivering and confused little heap of human misery—flattened by the onslaught of insurmountable difficulties that were dumped on him from seemingly nowhere to destroy his happy life.

But the healing of José was just as fast as the onset of his disorder. Not only did he come out of a healing session of some four and a half hours completely healed, José Goldblum, to this day, continues to astound those around him with the absolute pure genius of a brand-new and brilliant mind. It remains one of three or four of the most dramatic psychic healings George Barnard witnessed in his long and involved career as a mere-mortal helper in a platoon of Spirit Guardians. It also left him half blinded for days.

Better not try this at home.

They were soon to become a three-way partnership in the business of servicing the transport industry. One of them, an engineer, was an experienced technical man and George knew of him. The second partner was a professional administrator George had not yet met. The third was a sales and marketing man called Warren Mears. Barnard knew him to be a keen negotiator, reliable, a pleasant fellow with whom he had done some business in years past.

They seemed to have an ideal combination of skills and George thought their likely survival rate in business to be by far better than the average two-way, both-of-the-same-profession kind of partnership.

The launch of their enterprise was only weeks away and it had been agreed with Warren Mears that the Barnards' family business would support the new firm through its initial teething problems. George's specialized field of endeavor would also make him one of the partnership's major suppliers. They were counting on George's help, renting a factory in a nearby industrial estate, and already the Barnard teams were processing some of their smaller orders.

It was late on a Friday afternoon when Warren Mears telephoned. He was on the road, he said, selling up a storm. His partners were still in their old jobs, and all three wanted to see George on the following day, at the Barnards' home, to plan for the production of much work to urgently come George's way. Weekdays were still inconvenient to them.

George told Warren, "Saturday is fine. However, between eleven and twelve I'm taking care of a patient that looks a lot prettier than you do, Warren. Ladies first. But bring as many partners as you like after twelve. Have an early lunch with my family and me, and I'm all yours after that."

So it was arranged.

All three were just arriving as patient and therapist left the clinic. Warren Mears did the introductions, and then he said, "I know you're damned good at what you're doing, and now I find you're a shrink as well."

It was a quick, aggressive statement, and Barnard was more than a little peeved about what Mears had said.

So often, people most in need will rubbish those involved in the mental health professions. Those who are fine will generally just accept the practitioners for who they are. And fear, most likely and most often, may well be the cause of the scorn so glibly expressed.

"I'm not a psychiatrist," George told Warren bluntly, "I'm a clinical hypnotherapist, if you must put a ticket on me. And I have the uncanny ability to reach into my patients' minds, know their talents and weaknesses, know how they feel, what they did, and why, and therefore know how to help them shape their all-important future."

The aggressiveness of his rapid and lengthy response shocked even the therapist. What bothered him most was that it was simply not true what he had said. It was a myth, and it had seemingly come from nowhere.

It was rare for George to suddenly sense the whole picture, to feel how the patient felt, and know the cause and the cure. He certainly wasn't using it as an everyday tool. This kind of information did arrive in his mind, but only on rare occasions, and only when badly needed.

But as George looked him in the eyes, and as Warren stared back at him, the therapist "soaked up" all Warren's pickled old sins. All his bothers of half a lifetime ago were simply emitted from poor Warren's mind. George "read" what Warren had been up to in his younger years, and it wasn't very good.

Barnard didn't want to know all that. He got it all the same. And Mears knew the therapist had picked his brain. He was nervous, and quickly avoided Barnard's eyes. Too late, Warren, old boy, George thought. Perhaps some day, you will be my patient. That might be it. We'll be off to a flying start.

They got down to lunch and business after that, and George gave his ridiculous statement and Warren Mears' depraved past no more thought. The therapist had seen it all before—another sad re-run of the same old movie with a slightly different cast.

Months down the track it all became clear to Barnard, and by that time the new partnership was running routinely. Barnard received another call from Warren Mears, late one afternoon at his home, and smack in the middle of dinner. Warren sounded most upset.

"George," he said, "a good friend of mine is in deep, deep trouble. He looks like a ghost, he's talking rubbish, and shaking like a leaf. He's frightened of himself. He's got all these guns, hunting rifles, and I think he's going to blow his brains out. You've got to help him! Fix him up."

"If you think your friend is suicidal," George told him, "and if you are in fact right about that, he's beyond my help, Warren. Get this through your skull, old mate. He needs psychiatry, for sure. I'm in no way qualified to do anything for that boy. Take him to Casualty at District Hospital or St Clare's and they will give him a shot to calm him down till they find a psychiatrist to straighten him out."

"They'll kill him!" Warren answered with great conviction.

"They'll save him," George replied. "Or have you, perhaps, suddenly acquired all the needed qualifications to make a diagnosis of this magnitude?"

"They'll kill him!" Warren insisted. "Please, George, please! Please don't ask me how come I know, but I know. They'll kill him!"

Barnard tried once more to convince Warren, and in the most unkind of terms he could think of, that Mears didn't know what he was piffling on about, and to take the chap to the hospital. Quick smart, before it was too late. Mears kept on about not knowing why he knew, but being sure about what he was saying. His friend would die in the hospital, long odds-on.

Suddenly, George remembered what had happened just before that Saturday lunchtime meeting, and how he had picked Warren's brain. Again, he saw it all. Suddenly, he sensed it was never meant for him to know all of Warren's moldy old trespasses. It was meant for Warren to know George could sometimes actually do it.

There was nothing logical about this sudden revelation. It was simply there! It was undeniable! There was no more doubt about this than there was about George's poor dinner getting cold, and his not looking forward to a heavy evening session.

"Bundle him up in your car," George told Warren. "Don't let him drive. Keep him warm and be prepared to stick around all night to take him . . . God knows . . . wherever."

Warren Mears introduced the man. "George, this is José Goldblum. He comes from South America. Some thieves got into his business premises and stole all his goodies. But as soon as the insurance company paid up and he bought new stock, he got done over again. But now the insurance company won't replace anything, because there was a delay with the installation of new burglar alarms they had insisted on. José is now broke. He has lost everything, his house, his car, everything."

Barnard had seen the Goldblum store. It would have easily contained half a million dollars worth of high-tech computer, radio and other electronic gear, probably more. Some of George's Spanish patients knew and respected José. Goldblum helped people, advised his countrymen.

George shook Goldblum's hand and asked him some questions. The man was hard to understand, confused, hesitant. One needed to get used to his accent, and disregard the Spanish and even some German that "shone" through his stop-start English phrases.

Warren Mears said, "Well, George, you don't need me any more. See you later." He was out of the place like a flash, driving off with one of his partners and leaving Goldblum's car in the drive. Poor Warren Mears was spooked and could handle no more.

Barnard took Goldblum into his living room. The clinic was hardly the place for the man at that stage. They needed to have a quiet chat, not a professional interrogation, as this patient might perceive it.

George asked the man some simple questions, but something was happening to the answers that came. José was giving him three, or four, or five answers to each question, and not one of the answers was complete. It seemed he was searching the hemispheres of his brain in turn. His answers were switching from the factual to the emotional, with nothing in between. He would not present the simplest of problems to both hemispheres, so they could function in unison, and begin to solve the problem. That's how the therapist visualized it.

That's a Dissociative Reaction, George thought, then he almost immediately discarded the idea. Or a severe Anxiety Reaction? he wondered. No. That isn't it either.

Oh, Christ! This is a fresh-of-the-shelf, and virulent Post Traumatic Stress Disorder. And it might well be of a most complex nature.

He was sure of it now. The chap would be signing up for a long-term treatment, and not in George's clinic. He needed a more experienced mind than Barnard could provide. But George would try to settle him down, and ferry him off to St Clare's, later, much later.

He made Goldblum a drink and seated himself across the coffee table from the man. He watched him drink some of the coffee and said, "How do you feel, José?"

"I fear!" José answered. "Scared out of my weets!"

"Of what are you afraid, young man?"

"I don't know!" Goldblum answered. He took his time to look around the room as if he had not noticed anything in the place. "I see nothing here that frightens me," he suggested. "All se same, I'm scared. A fear, a fear, a fear . . . search me. Why should I be scared?" he asked George with great expectation on his face. The concept of his being so full of fear seemed ridiculous to Goldblum. And if it weren't so troubling, it would almost certainly be funny. "Do you know?" he asked hopefully.

Perhaps he thought his therapist would have that simple answer written down somewhere, in a book, under F for fear. The therapist could look it up for him, explain to the patient what it was, and that would clear that problem out of the way once and for all. José would then happily go home and that would be that.

One could jolly well read it on his face. "What you think, Meester? Goldblum is *never* afraid!" Here was an energetic, highly motivated businessman, who daily worked his way through a mountain of work, come to a grinding halt on a dead-end side-track of his life. Nothing of the buoyant, get-it-over-and-done-with personality was missing, but his mind had taken a wrong turn and lost itself, no doubt of that.

"Maybe I gone koo koo?" he suggested. He suddenly looked worried about that idea.

"No, José," George told him, "You are definitely not crazy." The therapist's casual remark seemed to cheer him up a little. He visibly relaxed and appeared to notice his coffee for the very first time. He checked the level of the brew, felt the warmth of the cup, and decided it was his coffee. Typical of PTSD and associated memory failure, pure logic was telling him there were two people in the room, that the therapist was holding his own cup, the other was his. It had to be! He knew Barnard would never be so rude as to make two coffees for himself and none for his patient.

It was also the third time he was studying the exquisite print on the porcelain cup with great care—another obvious symptom.

"Listen to me now, and stay with me, José," George told him. "You've been through a lot. You are probably too damned intelligent to go for a cop-out cold, a freaky temper tantrum, a cross-eyed migraine, or a phantom backache. But you must abreact the trauma in some way. Now you've got yourself a fear of a fear of a fear and you don't even jolly well know which way to run from it. That's a novel thing to do! I'm ever so proud of you for thinking that up all by yourself. It's a flippin' beauty!"

Goldblum was laughing about what George had said, but it didn't make his problem go away. It did, however, settle him down. He had looked ill and drawn on arrival. There was now some color in his cheeks, some light in his atypically blue South American eyes, an occasional, embarrassed smile.

"I'm going to ask you some questions now, José," George told him. "And I want your concise answers. Now! Every time you skip the answer, I'm going to ask you the very same question again. Every time you slip out of my clutches, you renegade, I'll grab you and I'll stick your nose right back on that question. So, listen to this: What happened to your business, José?"

Goldblum appeared to be enjoying the conversation, the company, the light-hearted chat, but they were struggling. Barnard felt like he was hungry, but he had only just finished a big meal. His eyes hurt and he felt tired for no good reason.

"Tell me about the business, José, not about your brother if he lives in Argentina. You gave him no shares in your business? Good. Tell me about the business, José."

Ever so slowly, Goldblum's ability to concentrate improved a little as they battled on.

"Tell me later about your wife, José. I'm sure she's a good mother and that you love her. But she does not work in the business with you, does she? Right. Stick with the business, Son."

There was some progress with his ability to stay with it, but even the term "marginal" might have been an overstatement. Barnard was feeling faint.

"José, I'm convinced your children are lovely and well-behaved, as you say. But they are too little to serve the customers in this country," George suggested. "Stay with the business."

It was an all-out fight for his continued attention. Barnard's eyes felt strained.

"José, you are not running the business from your home, are you now? Fine! Later we talk about your home," the therapist suggested.

The eyestrain he was suffering from was alarming him. He could no longer focus on José Goldblum. His patient seemed to be wrapped in an all-over coating of mildly iridescent fog. Barnard was now feeling very ill. He might soon pass out on the carpet, right in front of this young man.

That would do this patient a helluva lot of good, his cynical mind told him. He'll be running down the road, screaming. Or grow an extra set of thumbs out of sheer fright.

For Jesus' sake, help me, George's mind pleaded with the Spirit Guardians. Then he realized they were already at work. That illusive Golden Light was all around José Goldblum. It was also touching the therapist.

Barnard was now practically blind. Something beautiful, unexpected and awesome, but also frightening, was happening. A healing. Enlightenment. A re-birth.

"Oh, God . . ." he mumbled under his breath. "Give this poor, innocent mammal a warning, why don't you?"

This strange and age-old phenomenon has many names. Its recipients may have always felt the need to speak of it in terms more descriptive of the ecstasy it brought them personally. And, perhaps, before the advent of electricity, the term

Fire, Flame, or Tongues of Flame, rather than Light would have been a more appropriate way to explain such wondrous events.

The great Blaise Pascal spoke of Fire, John Yepes, and Whitman. And for that matter, so did the leader of a nation, Moses, the prophet, Mohammad, Guru Nanak. Many others did. Today, most speak of the Light. Over the years, Barnard needed to, at least in his own mind, differentiate between the different phenomena; the Glow of the Golden Flame, the Great Master's Golden Flame, and the Ember of the Golden Flame.

Within hours of arriving at the Barnards' home, José Goldblum was to experience the full and exhilarating impact of the Great Master's Golden Flame and deservedly become one of the Creator's latest "bright boys."

José had no idea what was about to touch him, heal him, and change his life for all time. Neither did Barnard. At least, George wasn't certain, and he didn't really dare trust his luck. He was hoping, praying for help and only briefly, before he lost all consciousness of time, place, purpose and self.

It turned out to be a Christmas present in the spring for one lucky, but deserving Argentine!

6

The Great Master's Golden Flame

"Homo sapiens" mind can probably not survive for long without being associated with a living brain," Barnard suggested to Veronah Miller, "That's if it can survive at all. But I can't see the mind as a mere force, simply generated by the brain. I astral travel, like millions of others do, and take my conscious, reasoning mind along with me, not my brain. I leave that organ safely tucked away in my skull. But the mere fact that mind cannot be seen, touched, or weighed on a set of scales does not mean it does not have form. It is the anatomy of the human mind that interests me, Veronah."

The practicing psychologist was sipping at the straw in her lemon squash. She nodded and vaguely gestured for the clinical hypnotherapist to go on. Minds did interest Veronah, but Spirit Guardians would always remain a big, fat joke to her.

"With nothing else to go on, let's model it on the brain," Barnard suggested. "Especially since brain and mind function so well in unison. Brain is likely to be the first or initial aspect of the brain/mind partnership. The brain of a frog will not support a sufficiently complex mind that will allow the amphibian to go and fetch a stick for you. The brain of one of your cats will not support a sufficiently complex mind for the feline to knit you a scarf, unravel it perhaps. But the human brain with all its intricacies can malfunction. And most of what we know about it, we've learned by observing physical trauma to, or degeneration of, specific parts of the organ, like a forceful blow to the back of the head can cause blindness."

"Yet your patient may wake up in the morning and think the curtains are closed. It takes him time to realize his sight has gone. His mind still knows how to look around, but his damaged brain is no longer doing its part of the job. One segment of his brain is dysfunctional in an otherwise healthy brain."

"Now apply the same concept to a severe blow to the psyche. There remains a perfectly healthy brain, but a segment of the mind has become dysfunctional."

Veronah gave the concept some thought. "What happens in your book to someone's mind when they're suffering from Alzheimer's?"

"The mind is constantly less capable of function as neuron breakdown progresses. The mind I visualize to exist in progressive/interactive segments, let's call them that, should be able to function less and less with that failing brain. But it should fail in distinct stages. The reverse is also observable in the way an infant is capable of organizing its brain/mind capacity to roll over, crawl, pull itself up with the support of a chair, walk, and finally start grasping the theory of relativity, rarely the other way around."

"George," Veronah suggested with a sigh, "please don't suggest this to any other member of our Association. You'll be swinging from the gallows at the crossroads by dusk of tomorrow. What on earth are you basing this theory on?"

"The sudden absence of a specific mind function after equally sudden psychological trauma and the sudden acquisition of additional mind capability in the process of Spiritual Illumination."

Barnard and Miller had been discussing one of Veronah's severe cases of PTSD. It was a tough case, which had so far failed to respond to any treatment. Long ago, the two practitioners had spoken of the patient being the deciding factor in the onset of the disorder. So many of them knew precisely when things had become too much for them. When, with their emotions pushed beyond the limit, they had opted out, virtually embracing the disorder to enable them to "kind of survive." Both George and Veronah suspected the corpus callosum to be involved in blocking information between the hemispheres of the brain. It was known to be able to block physical pain. Why not emotional pain?

But right now, Barnard was coming up with the theory that a segment of the mind, not the brain could be blocked in its function, even be ejected from a group of interactive mind segments. It was all too much for Veronah.

She gave the therapist a tired look. "George, we're not going to discuss Spiritual Enlighten-ment," she answered at last, "and if we were, not here in the club with a gaggle of our members hanging around. As far as concerns the loss of a specific mind function, they do, at times, come back, you know. That's what we are there for, if you hadn't woken up to that yet."

"Can't eyesight suddenly return after suffi-cient regeneration of the neurons? Speech, when a tumor is removed? Mobility, when the pressure of a stroke is surgically alleviated? The mind as an organ of progressive/interactive segments, building blocks if you like, is still my favorite model of its anatomy. Brain and mind are so different and yet, perhaps also so alike. Help me thrash it out, Veronah. Keep it in the back of your mind, observe. The physiologists won't do it for us."

Veronah nodded. "I can't argue with the concept," she said. "It does fit. What makes you think of deep things like that? Heavens above! Do you actually lie awake at night conjuring up these theories, or does it come from your Spirits?"

In the ten or eleven years since that discussion, Barnard and Miller had made no further progress. Except for the theory that in severe psychological trauma the misplaced, lost, ejected, or dormant "progressive/interactive" mind segment might return with the use of an equal-force staged trauma. They both knew of specific occurrences. They decided, however, that neither of them could dislike anyone enough to further traumatize the already traumatized, simply for the sake of research.

They were healers, contributors, carers, and proud of their achievements.

But the decade-old idea of Homo Sapiens' progressive/interactive segmented mind was very much in Barnard's thoughts as he sat there talking to José Goldblum. He knew something was happening, a spiritual healing, no doubt. He had no idea what the extent of it would be.

Slowly it began to dawn on him that the way he felt was the way José had been feeling. Barnard had entirely taken onto himself this patient's physical symptoms. That's why the patient appeared to be looking so much better when George looked at him before!

George wondered what he looked like now. José was just sitting there, quietly, but it was hard to focus on him. It felt like the therapist was looking at him from the very corners of his eyes, with his head half turned away from José, straining to make out his features, when he was squarely facing this young businessman across the coffee table.

Why is he no longer answering my questions, George wondered ever so vaguely? That isn't a very polite thing for him to do! Then, slowly, the therapist realized what was happening. I'm not asking him any questions! There was no need for José to think about answers. All he had to do was listen to what George was telling him.

So, what am I saying to this man, Barnard wondered?

Suddenly, the therapist realized that his speech was ringing out clearly. José Goldblum was receiving the instructions he so desperately needed. This would put his life back in order. All of it was brilliant, so concise, so perfectly logical. But none of it was coming from Barnard's mind. As the therapist finally, slowly realized what was happening, he relaxed. He gave in. Someone with a mind, much greater than I am blessed with, has taken over, George vaguely realized. Whoever he is, he deserves to be in charge. I'll just sit here and say the words.

The entire process was interrupted when his children came into the room to bring him a goodnight kiss. The children never noticed a thing! As soon as they left, he heard himself talking again. It was so easy. Just let it roll, he thought. And slowly, his mindfulness of being in the room, being there with José, being responsible for the man's welfare, and having an awareness of the passing of time, evaporated. Barnard was as if in a light sleep, and for many hours.

Suddenly, José Goldblum lit up brightly and at that moment Barnard's full awareness returned to him. It was half past twelve in the morning! They both now realized they had been there for hours on end. It was a time of great excitement.

"You're all lit up!" George told the man. "Fantastic! José, compared to the one hundred watt ceiling lights, you're putting out five hundred watts! Easy! It's all around you and it's much more intense around your head."

"I know dees," the patient answered. "And I can feel eet too. Look at se hairs on my arms are standing up on end."

There was no doubt about this fellow being back in the land of rational thinking. But he looked a sight. The hair on his head was standing up and out like the bristles of a worn-out broom. Again and again, he kept smoothing it down, but it just kept popping up again.

"You are se professor," he informed George.

Barnard laughed about that remark. "I'm not a professor," he told him.

"In Argentina professor mean teacher," José explained.

"Not even was I your teacher, José," George suggested. "What you have heard on this night did not come from me." He momentarily wondered if he had been sitting there all night, nattering away in Spanish. Anything is possible. How would I know, he thought? At that time, there was no recollection about anything he could have told Goldblum. It might have been gibberish, though he doubted that very much. Barnard simply didn't know.

"How are you feeling now, José?" he asked. "Are you fine now?"

"Yes, I feel ter-ree-feec!" he answered. "I know ex-act-lee what to do! Thank you very much. I'm going home now."

George laughed about his spontaneous outburst. His last few words had come so fast! Speech, reminiscent of machinegun fire, he thought.

"No you don't!" he shouted at José. "Don't you *dare* leave! You're going to stay right here. I want to watch this Golden Light. And I don't want you out there looking like a flaming mobile streetlight. You'll get arrested, and chucked in the stockade."

"What happen to me, happen to you?" José wanted to know.

"Long ago, José. Long ago," Barnard answered.

"Eef you say it deed not happen," he answered with a smirk on his face, "I know dees already. It deed happen to you, too."

"I call it the Great Master's Golden Flame, a rebirth. What you were before, you no longer are."

José Goldblum made no comment, but decided to stay put. They talked about his home, his family, his plans for the future. He spoke very fast, but Barnard was to later learn he tended to always communicate in that way. José knew precisely what it was he was going to do. He knew how it would all work out. He knew unerringly what was going to happen in the years to come.

Someone had provided him with a concise record of the future—the concepts, or the pictures, perhaps—but Barnard would never know. Did he learn all that from my voice and someone else's mind, he questioned? I may never know the precise answer. Strangely, José refused to believe George had nothing to do with his being healed, other than his sitting there and being used for the purpose. He still refuses to believe it, even to this day.

Barnard had been almost completely blinded in the process, but now his sight was slowly improving. Within days it would be back to normal. The redness and inflammation did eventually clear.

José Goldblum looked so healthy now, like he had just returned from a few weeks snow skiing. After some twenty minutes, the Golden Light around him slowly dimmed. Shortly after, he drove himself home, convinced George Barnard had some unusual power of his own. To José, nothing supernatural had happened. Just a routine day at the office for his new "professor."

The guy is an absolute scream.

During the years that followed, Barnard treated many of this fellow's countrymen, all referred to him by their Don José. But George could never look any of them in the eyes until they were seated in the clinic's recliner chair. The therapist learned that quick smart. They, also, were very cautious not to face the therapist until they were comfortably installed.

Before they arrived at the clinic, José Goldblum would hype them up to such a degree, they would simply fall down in a heap, anywhere, instantly, deeply hypnotized. José had made up his mind; it was all in the professor's eyes.

And no one dared question the great Don José.

Barnard was surprised to learn that José's banker had lent the man a six-figure sum of money. It needed to have been around half a million dollars at least, for José was deeply in the red at that time. The branch manager had not sought approval from Head Office either. That was a very risky thing to do. José had simply been extended the funds upon request, right there and right then. A handshake had sealed the deal. That was all. He was now running three separate new businesses, working tirelessly and for long hours. "No time for social veeseets," he told Barnard. "Making plenty money, Meester!" George knew he would be. The Great Master of this universe had showed him how to do that.

And there is no better Professor to be found.

Some years went by, and Barnard had moved to a new and bigger factory, but Goldblum quickly tracked him down. He had something to tell the therapist that just couldn't wait. His accent was as thick as ever.

"Eh, Professor Georgee!" he said, "Dees ees José Goldblum!"

Barnard burst out laughing. "I would have never known if you hadn't told me, José," he laughed. He simply couldn't help himself in responding the way he did.

"Can you guess what I just deed?" Goldblum put to him.

"How would I know what an Argentine gets up to?" George asked in return. "Anything at all could be expected."

"I just paid se bank eighty-three dollars and forty-two cents."

"You *did,* José? How kind of you! But I think it's hardly generous, my friend."

"I know dees. I know dees already," he suggested. "But you see, eet is se last eighty-three dollars and forty-two cents."

He had entirely cleared his debts, and had always looked forward to the day he could advise George of that victory. By this time, Barnard had long ago remembered some of the advice that came Goldblum's way—that many miracles were possible in the Great Master's universes. Sadly, there was little else he could recall. That lengthy, hours-long message was always for Goldblum, not for his therapist.

In the days immediately following Goldblum's promotion into the ranks of Graduates of the Great Master's Golden Flame, his energy was phenomenal. It had also gone wild, uncontrollable. He again came to see George, four, perhaps five days after the event, a little sad about having lost some close friends.

José had been talking to them in their kitchen, whilst leaning against the bench top. All of their expensive table silver lay curled up in the drawer. His merely being near it for a time had wrecked the lot.

"More than one tousand dollar worth," José suggested. "Nothing broken. All going in circles, dees things." The superstitious couple had thrown him out their door, and crossed themselves as he walked off down their street. Likely, they thought José was possessed.

He picked up a stainless steel teaspoon and looked at George. "I show you dees?" he asked.

"Yeah. Sure! Go wreck that five-cent thing," Barnard invited him.

Nothing happened for at least two minutes, and then it flipped over in his hands. Just like that! The therapist had never seen that done by anyone who wasn't in a deep trance. It really excited Barnard, but it didn't impress José.

"Perhaps I should hypnotize you, José," George suggested. "You may be able to control it better under hypnosis. It could be useful. You're doing precisely what Yuri Geller does for a living!"

Goldblum wouldn't hear of it. This strange, unwanted ability was going away now, thanks to "se Dear Lord," and he didn't mind losing the power. He knew precisely what he had to do, and bending spoons wasn't it.

Wine bottles had rocked on the shelves as he came near them, and both the refrigerator and the washing machine had "gone for a walk" in his presence. It had bothered him for days, and he was sick of it, spooked by it.

During the following days, José spent much time at the Barnards' home. He worked around the homestead and yard all day, and on any obvious project he could find. To some degree he unnerved the therapist. There was the possibility that the sudden healing had also caused a major new problem.

This fellow might be identifying with his healer in a most powerful way, George thought, wanting to be like me, perhaps even wanting to live my life for me, as a result of the shock to his system, however positive that shock had been.

Identification of that kind was hardly uncommon, but the therapist could have saved himself the worry.

"Everything feeneeshed," Goldblum came to announce, "what I can see. I go home now, George."

"Thank you, José," Barnard told him. "But you know, you really owed me nothing. You paid me for your consultation, and honestly, I just sat there and did nothing. Nothing much. A great battalion of Spirit Guardians put your mind back in order. All I did was ask for their assistance."

"Every day I hear dees," he answered the therapist. "You owe me nothing. You owe me nothing. I know dees. I know dees already. You say I owe you nothing? Okay! I owe you nothing. Nothing to you. But I owe. I owe and I must pay. For a great Gift, I owe a debt. Nothing to you, but I must pay."

He paused and looked his therapist in the eye, a wide grin, stretching from ear to ear. That grin told Barnard he was trapped, tied up, and soon to be roasted over a slow fire. "Nothing to you," Goldblum repeated deliberately, "but I must pay. So, I seelect you to pay dees debt to, because you help many others."

Don't argue with an Argentine. You can't ever win.

José Goldblum runs a business, just one business now. Those of his employees who hail from his part of the world know there is something special about their employer. They know that long ago something changed in him. They now call him Don José.

His friends, too, all know that one José Goldblum vanished way back then, another José Goldblum returned—a smarter, more caring, more thoughtful José. But he doesn't want to hear about the Great Master's Golden Flame, or talk about Spirit Guardians. Telling him about it is a waste of time. It is all in that Professor's eyes, you see?

The seemingly easy solutions to complex problems that flow from his incredible new mind now rate him well and truly within the classification of genius. And perhaps our minds are really constructed of progressive/interactive segments, one of which got squeezed back in, the other, a brand-new gift of great value, was popped on top. It was the very least the Guardians could do for one of the most deserving of contributors Barnard met in his life.

Goldblum still owes his therapist nothing, and he "knows dees already."

7

"A Favored Child You Are"

They said their prayers before meals. Their Papa usually led those prayers in his everyday gravelly voice that demanded much respect from all his brood. The children prayed with their eyes closed to better concentrate. Well, or else.

Occasionally, their Mama insisted on saying the prayers, for there would be something on her mind. Those were the times their seven children would watch Papa from the corners of their eyes, as he flinched when she stated her case.

"Dear Little Lord . . ." her prayers would begin. It was a term of endearment in her people's ancient dialect.

Though many would believe she might never visualize Joshua Ben Joseph as any taller than a six-year-old child, which was hardly the case. She knew Him well. They were the best of friends. They were in business together, somehow.

"Dear Little Lord, for the excellent meal set before us, we are truly grateful. We also thank Jehanne for her cooking." And at that point the only girl in the family would simply glow with pride, as a well-deserved compliment came Jéjé's way.

"But whilst we have Your attention," and this would be the point at which Papa would begin to flinch, and frequently cover his eyes, "there is Mrs.

Dordrecht across the way. We think she has suffered from her terrible asthma for long enough. A
. . . men."

She was a true daughter of the Ancients—
the blue-eyed, blond-haired people of the coast—
boat builders and fishermen who never minced
their words. She was a psychic at her people's
beck and call. She was a contributor.

"One of these days," her fun-loving children
often remarked in private, "Mama will tell the Dear
Little Lord He had better, for He owes her plenty,
and then some."

She never did. She stated her case in the
ways of the Ancients. She got results.

This would be her final trip to a land far away. She
was in her eighties now, and she was in pain, dying. But
they were relaxing on the sun-drenched patio, laughing,
talking about the past, and waiting for the children to
come home from their high schools.

It seemed there was a need for her to offload much
of what was saved up over the years—a favored life she
called it—of poverty and depravation, enemy occupation
of her ancestor's lands, the loss of a child and her man.

Talking to a therapist seemed to make her task a little easier. Another glass of wine helped her along.

"Do you still talk to the Angels and the Saints," she
wanted to know?

"They were due here this evening for dinner," he
answered her. "Told them all, 'Sorry Guys, an overseas
visitor. Grab yourselves some fast food.'"

She was laughing again, hurting, but laughing. "George, you'll never change!"

"They were the people who brought me up. Savages, I think. Heathens."

There was an important story coming. She was ready now, still smiling.

"I never told anyone about this. People might not have believed me. But I want to tell you now, for you know I wouldn't fib when I'm old and on my way . . . All those years, it has meant so much to me, George, but I kept it to myself."

He only nodded for her to go on.

"Your grandma died when she was still very young. In childbirth, but not really. Some days after. Then there were eleven of us, including the new baby. And I was not yet twelve, the third eldest, and I looked after everything in the house, cooking, washing, the little one, and sometimes even the store. The bigger kids were on the land, and the sea. There was so much land, and so many different crops. Peas and beans, and . . . Well, you know all that. And one day, they were all home from school and from the acres, and the girls were skipping their ropes in the yard, and I wanted to go out there, too."

She paused. Some tears had sprung up in her eyes, and she was somewhat embarrassed about it. Long-repressed needs still bothered her.

"Go on," he told her. "Don't go all soggy on me now, eh?"

"I wanted, too, to skip my rope! But I was so-o-o tired. Day after day, all that work, George, and no school for me anymore. I had my rope with me in the kitchen, but the potatoes were just about on the boil. That . . . happened so many times! And you know what children are like, don't you? They need to play sometimes. I was no different. But for me there was never time to play. And St. Christopher came along. And he lifted me up. And I skipped my rope in our kitchen. And I didn't have to hop up and down even."

It was the therapist's time to laugh. "He's got to be the most overworked Saint in the galaxy! Eh! Mom! He's got an office job now! Too old for that kind of caper."

She wasn't giving in too quickly. "He loves us seafaring people, always did, and he kept us safe from storms!"

Barnard shook his head. "You were most favored by one of my Friends, les Mill-Cent-et-Onze, the One, One, One, One, the Eleven-Eleven. Ask your grandchildren. They'll soon tell you. I'm not pulling your leg, but I just love . . . your story."

She still doubted his words. "How do they do that then? How do they get their feet out of the way? He was holding me up, but the rope never hit his feet, and I've been wondering about that for years. How does he do that?"

"Easy! They all have little wings on their shoes!"

"Now you *are* pulling my leg!"

"Yeah. And I don't know how they do it, but they can do it. They are very clever. And it might not have been a he. It could have been one of the girls."

"Girls?"

"Yes. Ladies. And they are very pretty. Beautiful! Can you tell me when it was? When it happened?"

"Late in the afternoon. Going onto sevens, I suppose."

"No. I mean what year, Mom. Roughly?"

"When I was thirteen, I think."

"That makes it nineteen-sixteen. Around that time?"

"Or a bit sooner."

She seemed to suddenly relax. That secret had inexplicably weighed heavily on her mind, and since her arrival almost a week prior to that sunny afternoon. The Spirit Guardian's student knew who had pressed her into telling him. He needed to know. It was part of his education. There would soon be another advance announcement of that kind.

From her teen years onwards, she had known she would have a rather big family. Quite inexplicably to her mind, she had also known one of her children would converse with St. Christopher, the "Big Man" in the town. Now she also knew who had lifted her high to skip her rope, but she was doubtful, still. It was to be read on her face all evening.

"Ask the children," he told her gruffly. "The kids all know."

"What do you think of it, George?"

"Une mémoire bien gardée. Secretly kept spiritual gold. A carefully hidden psychic gem, lady. A favored child of His you are."

"The Dear Little Lord is keeping me here for too long," she complained later that evening. "And I still miss your dad, you know? After all those years. I'm ready to go now, actually."

"He needs you here! Haven't you woken up to that yet?"

She eyed him with suspicion, smilingly, but knowingly. "How's that then?"

"If you go, there will be no one left on earth to tell Him what to do!"

She left for the Mansion Worlds just two months later, with "wings on her shoes." She is a true daughter of the Ancients.

8

Jasmin Chand Singh

The little girl with long, pitch-black hair walked right up to George Mathieu who was leisurely inspecting the family's back yard vegetable garden and smoking a cigarette. This miniature version of Jasmin Chand Singh, mother of two, was glaring up at George with a disapproving look in her big, deep brown eyes.

"Smoking is bad for your health," she warned the grown man in a most genuine tone of voice. "It will hurt your lungs and then you die."

"Yeah!" George agreed. He found it difficult not to smile at that sincere remark. "How old are you, nipper?" he asked. "Bet you don't know," he teased.

"Four-and-a-half," she answered immediately. "And you had better put out that cigarette and come inside. There will soon be food on the table that you have never tasted before."

Here was a smart little girl, telling him what to do and when to do it, and on his first visit to her home. But Barnard was not about to stub out his smoke yet. "So, all right then. You do know how old you are," Barnard grudgingly conceded. Then he added, "Okay. Fine! I can live with that. But I bet you don't know your date of birth."

"I . . . do . . . so!" was her response. And then she told him the precise date and time.

"You are a twenty-two master number," George told her after a quick calculation. "It gives me exceedingly great pleasure, Miss Chand Singh, to inform you that you are a very important person."

"I know that!" she responded with an air that implied he should have instantly perceived that obvious fact on arrival at her home.

He stubbed out his cigarette and smilingly followed the cute little muppet to where the food was waiting.

The muppet was right. George, indeed, had never tasted any of those dishes. They were spicy, but they were good.

An even smaller version of Jasmin Chand Singh had been watching George Mathieu from the dwelling's window as he wandered around her garden. Barnard had looked up a number of times and noted the little one's keen, spying eyes following his every move. Surprisingly, she now chose to desert her parents at their end of the table to sit right next to him, sparing him a big grin each time he glanced down at her. Here was an alert, daring, sociable and fun-loving little kid.

"I am much, much bigger than you are," Barnard informed her of the obvious, and with a smile he tried to elicit a response from her.

"Yes, you are," she agreed, so clearly spoken for one so young.

"Might you perhaps know how old you are?" Barnard asked. "I should think you do not know, but perhaps . . ." He was enjoying the interaction with this wise, confident little girl. So was everyone else in the room.

All eyes were on the child as she placed her spoon on the table and held up three stubby little fingers for all to see, then she pulled one finger down and gave her logical account for that unusual move. "Nearly three," she explained.

"Eight weeks to go, George," Jasmin chimed in with a laugh. "We sometimes suspect she may be counting the days. There's a new three-wheeler bicycle coming to make her acquaintance on her birthday."

Barnard was rather surprised by the ability to communicate of one still so tiny. He hesitated to pose his next question, not wanting to hurt her feelings. "I don't even know my own date of birth," he confessed, trying hard to show an honest face, "I forgot. It's long, long ago. So, I suppose you could be forgiven for not knowing yours."

Amazingly she understood, and knew the date, the year as well. Even more remarkably, here was yet another twenty-two master number, and with a configuration of numbers much like that of her older sister.

"You, young lady," Barnard explained to the child, "are also a very, very important person, just like your sister."

The child instantly agreed, nodded vigorously, and rewarded him with another big smile. But Barnard had long ago done the parents' numbers, and what struck him most of all was that the children's configurations had nothing in common with either Jasmin's, or her husband's. They could be throw backs to the grandparents, he mused.

Soon, the meal was finished. A notepad and pen were found, and Barnard poured himself over the figures.

The birth dates of both sets of grandparents were known and could easily be related to their respective children—the girls' father, and their mother. But both kiddies had nothing in common with any of their four grandparents either. It seemed the girls didn't belong to the family, but they surely belonged together.

Jasmin seemed to discern Barnard's inability to make sense out of the numerological Chand Singh family tree. "They are definitely ours," she explained with a nervous laugh, "not adopted."

Barnard threw the notepad onto the table, leaned back in the chair, but kept staring at the numbers. A pair of twenty-two master-number kids, in a two-kids-only family? And both of them all brain and mind, he mused? Nothing adds up. Ten, twenty thousand to one. Who knows? And the rest.

"They are very smart, Jasmin," he assured the mother. "They are all brain and mind. And if you think you know how smart, I'll tell you to forget everything you reckon you know about them. You've seen nothing yet."

What are these clever little babies doing here, he silently questioned?

"But for to teach the one who is to come!" came a loud voice. It was still ringing in Barnard's ear, but as always, no one else had picked up on it.

No one ever flaming well does, he angrily reminded himself! Settle down! Relax. He did, and then he was seeing the child.

There stood a little boy, about four years of age, waiting for Jasmin to take him to playschool. There was a full-color image of the child, projected across the low table.

"All brain and mind?" Jasmin remarked. She grabbed up the note pad and asked, "Do you mean the numbers you've circled here? George? Eh, George!" And as Barnard finally nodded that it was so, she said, "They're all circled!" Then, more pensively, "They should have been boys."

It seemed girls weren't required to have brains and minds, according to the mother. There was no mistaking her heart-felt disappointment at her not yet having borne a son. It was something George Mathieu would never understand, but he knew that for whatever reason, it was typical of her race to want boy children.

"Your next child will be a boy," Barnard promised her calmly.

There was an instant look of agony on Jasmin's face, no response.

"Suit yourself, girl," Barnard told her. "I just saw him, clear as day."

She suddenly looked hopeful, intrigued. "Are you sure?" she asked.

It was Jodi Barnard who answered her in his stead. "George never misses, Jasmin. And you don't have to be pregnant for him to see the next child. It works all the time. He doesn't even know how he does it, but he does it. And because he's scared stiff of babies, they're always showing up at two, or three years of age." She was rubbing it in, ready to let him have more. "He won't touch them until the fragile labels fall off them at eighteen months. But I have always had that suspicious feeling it might have more to do with him not wanting to change their diapers."

Jasmin had heard enough. "You saw him at two or three years old?" she wanted to know.

Barnard shook his head. "Four. Four years old. Off and on his way to playschool, Jasmin. But before he gets there, he will already have had two teachers. His sisters. They will literally hunt up his IQ to an unbelievably dizzy height. Those two are born teachers." It was all so clear in Barnard's mind, and so fast.

Soon after, they left the Chand Singh's. Barnard had not been prepared to tell the woman that the son she had not yet conceived would become an enlightened one. He might or he might not tell her later. He would certainly have to inform her the child was to be educated along the strictest of their religious teachings. He was under no circumstances prepared to inform the mother-to-be that her child would communicate with the 11:11 Spirit Guardians. Her boy would become a rookie in a progress platoon, no doubt of it. ABC-22 already knew and had passed on the information in a flash.

Barnard had no idea it would be almost six years before Jasmin's little boy made that first great journey to his playschool just five doors down his street. As the months ticked by, Jodi Barnard kept informing her husband that their friend, Jasmin Chand Singh, was stubbornly "refusing" to fall pregnant.

"Did you see it all wrong, then, George?" she wanted to know.

"No," he told her. "It'll happen. But what puzzles me is that the information arrived so far ahead of the event and so effortlessly. Think about it. The Guardians needed to practically sell their souls to find out about Michael's drowning at that beach whilst we would have been in the

Philippines. And that was to happen only a few weeks into the future." He gave her a searching look. "Do, Jodi, please, occasionally rub a few cerebral neurons together till you get a mild spark and think about that proposition."

"I don't think about those spooky things," she answered smugly. "That's what I married you for. No other reason. *You* think about it."

"I did. And I've concluded that the administration of this local universe is another of those bureaucratic nightmares," Barnard contended. "All red tape. Everything is on a need-to-know basis for the evolutionary two-legged mammals."

It was clear she didn't believe him.

"It's true, Jodi! And for every new concept that falls within our grasp, some bunch of devious Seraphim invent two more enigmas, stick them into folders, glue them shut, and mark them "secret and confidential." We're here for no other purpose but to entertain their perverse natures. This world is their sadistic equivalent of a mind-game fun park, and interactive zoo."

"You can be so . . . Oh, I don't know."

It was Saturday, and early breakfast time in the Barnard household. The three white-haired, blue-eyed Barnard offspring were noisily devouring their scrambled eggs, toast, and jam.

"Jasmin is back in the hospital and this time they are keeping her there," Jodi Barnard informed her husband. "She still has more than a week to go, supposedly. That makes this the fourth false alarm. Wouldn't you get fed up with it?"

"I have no immediate personal reference to the problem of childbirth," Barnard suggested dryly, evasively. Seven o'clock was much too early for him.

The children were laughing. Jodi ignored his remark. "Jasmin hasn't even had a scan or anything, so they don't actually know if it is a boy or a girl. She's confident, though. But if it does turn out to be a girl, she says, we can have it."

Barnard looked around the table, carefully studying each of his children in turn. "Okay," he agreed at last. "You'd never tell it apart from these, our own crowd."

The children thought that was funny as well. Jodi had nothing to say. She was on her way to answer the homestead's noisy telephone. Moments later she was back.

"That was Jasmin! And she's got a boy! And everything is fine. The baby weighs . . ." She seated herself again. Then her mouth fell open and she stared at her husband in disbelief. So she stayed.

"Don't just sit there sitting there," Barnard suggested with a measure of annoyance in his voice. "What, Jodi? That baby weighs . . ." he repeated. "How much does the thing actually weigh?"

The children were laughing again, and Jodi finally discovered her tongue. "George? Jasmin said she was going to telephone her husband next up. She phoned us first! She let us know before anyone else! She wanted *you* to know! Do you realize what it must have meant to her, for you to tell her? All that time . . ."

"How much does it weigh, woman?" Barnard was getting impatient with her.

"We'll have to go and see her now!" Jodi replied. "You will have to come, too, and the children. We'll all go. Jasmin would never forgive us . . ." She seemed to suddenly notice the wearied look on her husband's face. "Nearly eleven pounds and twenty-one inches long," she answered quickly, finally.

"Not worth bothering about," Barnard joked.

"That's big! Huge! He'll be even taller than his dad. You'll *have* to come with us, George."

Barnard shook his head. And with a wink directed at his children, he said, "I hate kids. Can't stand them! They clutter up people's houses. They're not really human."

There was a roar of laughter from the children at his remark. Years of jesting had made them utterly immune to that kind of preposterous statement. And they tended to often turn to their straight-laced mother to explain their dad was only joking.

Constant exposure to the profound, and the ridiculous, will develop their brains and minds, Barnard mused as he laughed with them.

But his crude jokes never did Jodi any good. She was angry now.

"You *must* come with us!" she insisted.

"I've got patients this morning, Jodi."

"Three hours from now!" she objected. "We'll be back by then, easy."

He shook his head and sighed. "Uh, uh! I can't go. There was an 11:11 courtesy wake-up call last night. Something serious is brewing and I'll have to be in the clinic."

One of our greatest intellectual deathtraps is our need for predictability. We feel safe when constrained by the self-constructed perimeter fence of our perceived arena of cerebral activity. We hesitate to move beyond those self-imposed and well-known mental boundaries that box us in.

To Barnard, the 11:11 courtesy wake-up call from the Spirit Guardians of the Halfway Realm meant for him to remain at home. Someone in need would call on him, and his assistance in his capacity as a practicing hypnotherapist would be needed. It was in his clinic where psychic events came about, spiritual happenings occurred, some patients even attained enlightenment. That was where, to his idle mind, things happened "all the time."

But did they? Really?

In reality, the preponderance of these psychic and spiritual events occurred outside the clinic, the lesser number within its walls. And those four walls constituted just another complete set of self-limiting boundaries of a big box within which he felt safe. Safe in the knowledge that there, and at any time he felt like being slothful, he could get away with not thinking beyond the square.

9

The Avatar

Barnard felt some concern for Jasmin Chand Singh, a lot more concern for Jasmin's marriage. Her husband could have been on hand for the birth, George felt. Surely, the man could at least have been notified before anyone else was told. Was their marriage under strain? It turned out not to be the case.

Not at all.

The therapist had greatly underestimated the enormous stress the woman had lived under for years. For her to bear a son, it seemed, equated with the fulfillment of her life's primary, if not only, goal. George's casual description of a four-year-old ready to go to playschool, followed by Jodi's assurance that these visions happened all the time, and could be relied upon, gave Jasmin faith.

Jasmin had lots of faith.

In the two years following the little man's birth, Jasmin and all her family would have to draw on the strength of that faith, and to its very limit. But once again, a new vision would help to give her and everyone in her extended family the capacity to endure what was to come.

"You *can't* stay at home, George," Jodi Barnard insisted. She wasn't giving up. "Jasmin is one of my best friends. What am I going to tell her? Sorry, mate, but my husband thinks he's much too small to bother about, and they all look like lumpy potatoes anyway?"

She ignored her children's chatter and laughter about lumpy potatoes. "Ask your Spirit Guides if you've got time to see Jasmin and be back in the clinic for whatever is going to happen," she snapped at him.

"Okay then," he mumbled. "You've won." He gulped down the last of his coffee and wandered off to the clinic, again forced to contact the Spirit Guardians when he had so often promised to give them a lengthy break.

But the Guardian, ABC-22 would not show up. There, in front of George Mathieu and a little to his right stood someone the mortal had never seen before. With great apprehension the rookie scrutinized the unexpected arrival.

He was a tall, white-bearded man in long, creamy-white, golden embroidered, flowing robes. There was a rather tall blue turban on his head to which was attached a shiny, metallic insignia. His hands, palms together, came up in front of his upper chest. Then he bowed his head ever so slightly, after which he straightened again.

Is that a greeting, a sign of respect, or both, Barnard wondered? The rookie wasn't used to Spirit Guardians showing him respect. Friendship was what the mortal always appreciated. An extremely rare but casual interchange of humor invariably made his day. Criticism is what he often deserved, and inevitably received.

Respect was what the greatly irreverent rookie neither showed, nor appreciated receiving, especially from One who so radiated intellectual and spiritual attainment, and who so far outranked him. The thought came to mind that this might be a Melchizedek, but the Guardians' student would never be sure, or ever find out.

Barnard was a businessman, industrious by nature, and that commerce-like attitude extended to his dealings with Spirit Guardians. There was rarely the time for niceties or socializing. There was ever another project to be businesslike about. There surely was a copious splash of inverted snobbery, as well. He was a human with an attitude.

Someone had obviously also neglected to inform this wise "Indian Man" that no Spirit found it easy to strike a bargain with George Mathieu unless the always still distrustful mortal knew precisely who he was dealing with, talking to, or working for.

"What's your name then?" Barnard asked, still uneasy about the unheralded intrusion of this stranger into his supposedly secured domain.

"Avtar," came the reply. It wasn't very clear at all. It could well have been, "Abtar."

It would do Barnard no good asking him to repeat that strange word. The "Man" with the turban had gone.

In his stead, but much more to the left, there suddenly appeared a big round smiling face Barnard knew very well. It was Sarasvati, near toothless grin and all. Recognition of the Swami's unusual features took Barnard only moments. Moments later the vision was also gone.

Then, right in front of the rookie appeared a deep-brown mud-brick wall. Glued to the wall were the roughly cut out, big, white paper letters that spelled the word, SARASVATI.

This vision wasn't about to disappear in a hurry. It stayed there for a long time. The sun appeared to be beaming down on this scene. A warm breeze was blowing. Slowly, one by one, the paper letters curled up in the breeze, then detached themselves from the mud and were blown away. The I was lifted off into the wind first of all. The T followed moments later. The A and the V almost took off together. The S, A, and R floated away in that order.

The whole name was disintegrating from right to left.

Perplexed at the strange vision he was having, Barnard expected the remaining two letters, the A, and the S, to fly away next and in that order. But they stayed right where they were. Then, suddenly, the whole vision was gone.

"That 11:11 courtesy wake-up call was in fact for Jasmin, Jodi," Barnard told his wife. "Something important." He paused. "Quite a few things of importance for the future, actually, and she needs to know about them. I'm coming with you guys. And you will need to give me some time with her."

Jasmin Chand Singh didn't look like a woman who had given birth, just a little more than an hour earlier. She was beaming, happy and proud of her accomplishment. And her new baby boy looked healthy. But with all the chitchat of praise and congratulations, it took some time for George to finally get her attention.

"Someone came to visit me this morning, Jasmin," he informed her with a laugh. "Someone with a big blue turban on his summit, and he said you are meant to give your child a name starting with S and A. I hope that makes sense to you. He told me a few other things, as well."

There was an instant look of amazement on the woman's face. Then came a smile that seemed to want to stay just where it was, forever. Something had obviously rung a bell. Finally she said, "I was always going to call him Sarjit. It's just in the last few days that my husband has thought of another name. We will call him Sarjit!"

"There was more, Jasmin," Barnard reminded her.

"Was it Guru Gobind Singh who came to see you?" she asked excitedly. "Or Guru Nanak?" Without being told, Jasmin had instantly presumed that the visitor was a Spirit Being.

"No," Barnard answered. "He had a rather strange name. And I didn't hear him too well. He said his name was either Avtar, or Abtar. One or the other. That's what it sounded like."

Jasmin was snickering. "Avtar, George! He was speaking to you not in English, but in my people's language. He was saying Avatar! He was an Avatar!"

Barnard had heard of Avatari, but long ago banished the concept to where he felt it belonged, in Hindu fairytales. Fundamentalist Christian teachings might still have had a powerful grasp on the mind of this helper of the 11:11. And maybe an Avatar was the very same creature as a Melchizedek. And perhaps the message was more important than the Messenger.

"Whatever, Jasmin. Whoever. But he was very intelligent. Absolutely brilliant! And he said your son will be deeply involved with medicine, specifically experimental medicine. Research. It will be his choice of involvement entirely. And he will be very, very successful at it. But he won't be in it as a member of a team, Jasmin. He will tend to be a loner."

Barnard gave her a detailed description of the clothing and turban with silver-colored insignia "Mr. Avtar" was decked out in. Jasmin recognized all three of these as having special reference to the precise location—a small district, village, or town—from which her grandparents hailed. It appeared to have been a very accurate psychic hit.

Barnard, however, wondered what was so important about the little man's name. Why Sarjit, he wondered? Who cares? Bruce, Freddie, Charlie, or Dennis would do.

As long as the little fellow is healthy, who cares?

Barnard would soon learn about what really mattered about Mr. Avtar's message.

Sarjit Chand Singh was not deserving of being graded a misshapen potato, or even a typical baby. Sarjit was undeniably a boy.

And his behavior as a ten-week-old caused both Jodi and Jasmin to remark that he must have got to know George Mathieu in a previous life. His alert eyes quickly picked Barnard out of a group of people and followed him around. He also promptly became attuned to Barnard's voice, even though he wasn't visited all that often.

But at six months of age Sarjit was hospitalized. Two days later, desperately ill, he was transferred to a specialist children's hospital. Shortly after, the specialist ordered his little body to be blasted with chemotherapy, again and again, with months, and then only weeks, between the heavy doses.

Soon, the little man found himself checked-out and prodded at by scores of specialists, all of whom would simply shake their heads. And by the time he was one year old, he was below his birth weight, unable to crawl, unable to sit up, let alone walk. But he hung in there, and rarely cried. He was tough. Brave!

And he was dying.

"They want to perform an operation on him," Jasmin informed Barnard on the telephone. "It's something altogether new. It has never been done before."

"What is the prognosis, Jasmin," he asked, deeply concerned, shocked and doubtful, and realizing too late he had posed a rather ridiculous question.

"Officially, chances are not good at all, but nobody knows," she answered. "Unofficially, he has a hundred percent chance of going to playschool when he's four, remember?" There was not a note of sarcasm in her voice.

Jasmin Chand Singh had faith, stacks of it, and much more of it than George Barnard ever had. She had left the glib-mouthed therapist speechless. The awful news had winded him.

She was still on the line, waiting for a comment from him that didn't come.

"Now he can be that loner in pioneer health care," she explained. "His choice altogether not to be part of the research group that will perform the operation," she suggested. "But he's doing all he can, the little loner, just staying alive." She was still waiting for him to say something.

"Yeah . . ." he answered vaguely, still in shock.

"Had you forgotten what you were told? George!" This sounded like a severe scolding he had truly deserved, not a question.

"I didn't think . . . never . . . not this way . . . but you're right, Jasmin."

"You were told he would be successful," she answered. "That's all I have to hang on to. God help us all."

"He will! We both already know He will."

The hospital staff didn't want to part with him after all that time. The nurses all cried when he finally left. He was their much loved miracle boy, who smiled even when in great pain.

At age four, and after a notable career as an irreplaceable collaborator with a medical research team, and a subsequent one-year-long "furlough" at the end of their successful project, he finally entered playschool, happy and healthy.

He is our Sarjit Chand Singh.

Will I ever know?

Was it incorruptible Faith,
   which brought the rewards of Spiritual Light
   and the Great Master's Golden Flame?

Or did so many weaknesses and failures of mortal life
   require the rescue packages of His great Gifts?

Will I ever know?

But as I search to discover,
   let me honor Regret, despise Guilt,
   and always have Faith.

part four

The "Loss of Status"

There was never any doubt about who owned and conducted the Barnards' family business. Even at its height, it still tended to be very much a one-man show. Kevin Weiss had his own, clearly delineated area of authority that Barnard would never interfere with. The firm's secretary, Lucie, was perhaps the most outspoken and contentious of all employees. She did not always follow orders, but likewise, she often did a lot more than she was asked to do.

Undisputedly, however, George Mathieu was in control.

In his clinic, questions needed to be asked of his patients. Their own responses allowed him to more clearly view their real needs. The appropriate questions at the appropriate times simply nudged them along, made them think more clearly, plan their own futures and their healing. The patients were in control at all times. Barnard would rarely make a forthright suggestion about their obvious next move.

As a therapist, he only mediated between their intellect and their emotions.

The terms of his treaty with the Spirit Guardians of the temporal Halfway Realm were never clearly elucidated. Nor were many of the countless misunderstandings between the Guardians and the mortal ever resolved in detail. The contact between the Guardians and their underling was hardly extensive. Much of what they had to tell him was lost through human conceptual poverty. There was no school, no classroom, not even an instruction manual for those who assist the Guardians.

There was just an opportunity, each time, for George Mathieu to blunder from one foolish presumption into the next.

Barnard had made the conscious choice to get involved in some way, but without knowing what he was in for. The genius-minded Spirit Guardians must have had a massively detailed psychological profile on the mortal—an assessment that would have made any therapist's mouth water. So, whatever could have possessed them to decide to enlist Barnard into one of their platoons?

He was an over-active, willful, proud and emotional creature. From the outset, he was likely to give them a lot more grief than pleasure.

He hated being dictated to. He detested being hampered in any of his projects. That, especially, could make him lose his temper. Their Celestial-Mortal Alliance would eventually fall apart.

It was bound to.

10

Jennifer Sutton

Spirit Guardians don't rebel. At least, George Mathieu Barnard truly believes they do not. But Barnard is only a common mortal, and by virtue of that fact, he tends to be a rebel.

The therapist boldly inquires why, in a so-called civilized world there is the pain of hunger, the scourge of disease, homelessness, joblessness, the loneliness of isolation. And he doggedly still demands to know why wars must be fought, crimes must be perpetrated, victims must suffer.

To learn? Learn what? Progress? Progress to where?

The Spirit Guardians, his Protectors and Superiors, so often answer his numerous questions by telling him, "This is meant to be," "This is the mosaic of your time," or, "It is so arranged."

Such vague answers do not allow Barnard to perceive the local universe as well-ordered, progressive or a beneficial place. Such answers explain nothing but chaos, the laissez-faire results of imperfect man wrongly entrusted to rule imperfect mankind's domain.

Barnard will not accept wrong as right, sad as happy, and broken as whole.

And this makes him a rebel.

All the Suttons' children were small and thin. It was bound to be genetic. Brian, the driving force behind Sutton Engineering Ltd, scarcely came up to Barnard's shoulder. Brian's wife, Emily, was a little smaller still.

One might suggest the Suttons made up for their lack of size in sheer numbers. The doting parents, at last count, were blessed with eight well-behaved children, of all different ages except for their five-year-old twins. How they all fitted into their old and tiny, bright-yellow cottage just down the road from the Barnards' homestead, and without there being regular fights, was anyone's guess.

But one of them was about to suddenly leave home.

The usually cheerful and outgoing Brian Sutton wore a concerned look when George Mathieu entered his premises. Barnard quickly dropped a heavy, bent and warped main driveshaft on the engineer's workbench. "Straighten her and harden her, Brian, if you can, please," he suggested. "A new one will cost us near enough four figures today. And it would have to come from interstate."

The engineer closed one eye and slowly rolled the shaft along the bench, feeling the movement. If anyone can fix that shaft, George thought, Brian Sutton can.

The engineer wasn't saying anything. The troubled look on his face remained. If it would take him longer than a day to fix the shaft, work would stack up high in Barnard's small plant. Two days, and they would no longer be able to breathe in the place. Production would come to a grinding halt.

Production *will* come to a grinding halt, judging by the look on his face, Barnard concluded. Why did I become a manufacturer?

"Nothing to it," said Brian. Surprisingly, he didn't look any happier. "You'll have her back this afternoon."

"What's troubling you?" George asked.

"It's Jennifer," the engineer answered. "She's been diagnosed with a hole in the heart. She must have been born with it and we never knew or suspected it, but she did always sleep a lot."

Jennifer was their third youngest, perhaps four years old and a happy child. She was the proud owner of the most enduring and infectious giggles of all in the Sutton family.

"You'd never ever have guessed that," George suggested. "They'll fix her up, Brian."

"Not while she's got that lung infection," the engineer informed him. "They won't touch her until the congestion has cleared."

"Where is she?" Barnard asked.

"At home again, with Emily," Brian sighed, "and, man, I just wish I could be there with the both of them."

I'll fix her, thought Barnard. I'll heal that little nipper tonight. He would never risk talking about his healing the sick at a distance. It turned some people off. It even tended to impede the work if others knew what he was doing.

"I'll fix her," he grunted to himself as he made his way back to his factory. He was determined to give Jennifer Sutton priority over everything else that evening. "A hole in the heart is kid-stuff," Teddy Willis had told him years ago. And Professor Dr. Edward Willis had forgotten more about psychic healing than Barnard would ever know. "You make like you're darning a sock, George.

You basically do the repairs on the patient's astral body. The physical body must follow its lead and heal itself. In two or three days the average hole in the heart will be closed. It never fails."

But Barnard wondered about a sudden empty feeling in his stomach. It was literally roaring for no good reason. More unsettling was the strange feeling that suddenly came over him. He actually felt like he could not care less about that precious little girl with the million-dollar chuckle.

"That isn't me! Disgusting!" he complained to his unseen Companions. "I love kids and Jennifer is special."

"One pint-sized Jennifer Sutton coming up," he told himself that evening in the darkened clinic. "Drift . . . drift . . . drift, George Barnard. Go down deep and reach out." He was simply repeating the words Ted Willis had always used. He could almost hear the old lecturer's voice still resonating in his ears, enticing his students, urging them to let the metabolic rate of brain and mind plunge.

"Aha! So, there you are, Kiddo. In real now-time."

She looked like a pale little doll, lost in a bed that seemed too large, in a room too cramped for a child. She was facing precisely northeast, propped up against her pillows and dressed in pale yellow pajamas.

Her breathing was shallow and labored. Above her left shoulder, the only small window of her room offered no more than a view of a blank wall of the unattractive residence next door. Not a glimmer of sunlight would ever dare to execute a break-and-enter into that room.

"Never you mind, puppet," the psychic mumbled. "Come on, up you get. Leave your body behind now and come to me. That's how it works." We'll have you out of here and in the sun and fresh air in no time flat, he thought. "Come on!"

She wouldn't budge. Her fairytale picture book slowly came to rest upside down on the sheets and her tiny hand dropped listlessly on its cover. Her head moved back against the pillows and her lackluster eyes slowly rolled up to stare at the ceiling.

Come on, Baby, nothing to it, his mind urged the youngster, but she remained the way she was—unaware of a presence to whom all others had responded when urged, and for so many years. That spark of life was gone from her, it seemed.

What is this, his mind demanded to know sharply?

"Not yours to heal," came ABC-22's immediate response.

"She's mine!" he loudly snapped at the Spirit Guardian. "She came my way, that makes her mine. It goes without saying. She's special, this little giggler, and she's mine."

"It is not meant to be," came the answer. Although hardly emotionless, his voice certainly sounded so very definite.

That can't be right! "I can do it without your help," the mortal mumbled. "I must, for Brian and Emily." Barnard was tired of blindly following the Spirit Guardian's orders. He was sure he could handle it by himself. Ted Willis had told him he could. Kid stuff, Willis called it. "And I have fixed up worse than this in the past, Bzutu."

He tried to cajole the youngster out of bed, but to no avail. She moved only slightly to his ever more desperate calls. He tried to reach out and touch her, but each time he felt himself being pulled back again. Then, with his hand only inches away from the dark fringe that curved onto her pale little forehead, Barnard was suddenly jerked back with force.

"Damn it all!" The instant flaring of his temper speared him back to the surface.

"Who decides what's meant to be?" he asked. "Who decides a kiddy like her isn't going to bloody well make it?" he wanted to know. "And who gives me this disgusting feeling like I don't even care about her? That isn't me!"

There was no answer. ABC-22 had left.

He found a jar of walnut colored wood putty and a sturdy palette knife in the cellar. "I'll get her tomorrow night, you'll see," he grunted defiantly under his breath. The lid levered off the jar with ease, and the putty was still viscous.

"It's just an off-day I'm having, that's all. I'll get her." He pushed a lump of putty into the bruised, soft timber wall and smoothed it with the blade.

"That's pleurisy, all that fluid in her chest. Too much of it around her heart as well, squeezing it. She's being choked."

He picked up the cigarette butts from the silver-blue carpet and swept up the ashes. His favorite ashtray, a most expensive birthday present, was broken, and quite beyond repair. "Cripes, I've got to learn to control that bloody temper of mine." Give up smoking? Nah. Not now.

Brian Sutton wandered into the plant at nine the next morning, "How's that shaft holding out?" he asked.

"Fine," George told him jokingly. "We managed to get it fixed at Sutton Engineering. They know what they're doing, if we don't. Sutton Engineering fixes all our mistakes. How's Jennifer, Brian?"

"She's great! She's resting quietly. Sleeping a lot, but picking up. No more fever."

She's given up! George's mind told him. My God, she's throwing in the towel. You'll have to heal the child tonight. "That's fantastic news," he told the father. He so desperately hoped it sounded convincing.

Yet, from that moment on, and during the many weeks that followed, the experience of little Jennifer Sutton was mysteriously lifted from his mind.

Driving past the Suttons' home on many occasions did not bring the attempted healing episode back to memory. Seeing their school-age children line up for their bus, similarly, did not give Barnard the needed jolt. It was as if to his mind the four-year-old had never existed.

So many things could have jogged his memory. An old, awkward little dish had replaced his wasted clinic ashtray. That could have triggered the right kind of thinking. The hasty repair job to the clinic's natural timber wall had dried up much too light. His patchwork looked positively revolting. Surely, it should have caused his brain to have a minor explosion smack in the right neuron cluster. But there was nothing.

Seeing Brian Sutton drive his pick-up truck into its parking space didn't revive the experience of coming so close and having almost been able to touch little Jennifer on the forehead.

It remains an isolated incident Barnard may never be able to explain. Regular meditation simply did not allow for a matter of such importance to disappear from his mind. But it did disappear from his mind, and perhaps it was truly stolen from his mind.

No other interpretation makes sense.

The memory of it all came flooding back like a tidal wave, a veritable killer-tsunami. "Oh, my God, no!" Barnard cried. "May the Dear Lord forgive me."

His foreman looked at him in surprise. "It won't cost us that much," the production man complained. "Jesus! It's a standard size bearing, George, and Brian Sutton might just have one to spare. It's going to cost us a lot more in my time if I've got to shop around for one."

"Borrow a hundred, Kevin," Barnard told him. "It's not what you were talking about, it's what you said. You reminded me of something—something totally unrelated. I should be keelhauled for forgetting . . . and shot right after for carelessness. No, it's not you. Go get your bearings at the Suttons' place. Forever! You're fine."

Kevin Weiss cautiously studied his employer. "You know, that took every last bit of color out of your face," he suggested. "Grab a coffee and a ciggie. Sit down for a bit. And don't tell me what you forgot." He left, muttering, "Talking about neurotic therapist-employers. Gawd!"

Still, there was a gap in George's recall of the events. It puzzled him. Now, what was the name of the Sutton child again, he questioned in his mind? He could clearly visualize the little sprite and he could name all the Sutton family, except their little four-year-old. How ridiculous! Finally, he remembered. Jennifer, of course! How stupid can you get, George Mathieu, to lose the kid's name?

"Perhaps there are sayings in the Halfway Realm, Barnard suggested cynically. Like: 'Any discussion of over ten words is not worth having.' Or: 'If you can avoid it, do not talk to humans.' But, of course, there's always: 'Although I hate your jokes, we can still be friends.'" Barnard was giving up on the Guides. "We could always correspond by mail if it suits you better."

The ancient mighty Warrior simply shrugged, then leaned more heavily on his spear. He was not amused by George's sarcasm. It was only a feeling that was being conveyed from the Spirit Guardian's mind. George knew the feeling only too well. It was the feeling he detested so much.

The feeling of not caring.

"Red, yellow, brown or white, Bzutu. Even those of your unusual shade of whatever—I love them all. And when they come my way, they're meant to be healed," he told the guardian. "It's called Barnard's Law. And all the kiddies on this planet are mine. This vertebrate claims all rights to those of his own species."

"Not yours to heal," came the impatient response. The blunt end of the spear almost touched the mortal's chest in a gesture to hold him back. The Guardian's sudden move shocked Barnard. He momentarily felt fear of the mighty weapon and was in two minds about going on with the healing.

"What the hell. I'll do it without your help," Barnard made his decision. Sheer pride forced him to stay with the plan. "Watch me," he told the Guardian. "I also have the power, and the free-will franchise, my Friend. I'll show you how it's done. You and Teddy Willis taught me too well. Now you're both sorry you did," he snickered. Instantly, Guardian and weapon faded. Moments later, Barnard was back in Jennifer's room.

The Suttons' three-year-old occupied Jennifer's bed. He was fast asleep, and sucking his thumb. George feverishly searched all the rooms, and some of them twice. But for Brian in his chair, Emily and their eldest son on a couch, all were asleep. There was no Jennifer.

She could well have gone to the hospital, the healer guessed. Catapulted into space above the darkened town, no telltale pinprick light told of Jennifer's presence in any of the town's hospitals.

Might she be staying with relatives, he wondered? Even before the outline of the Australian landmass was clearly in sight, he knew there would not be a tiny blinking light to guide him down to her.

Overseas for an operation, he guessed wildly? A frenetic search of the continents brought not a glimmer of light as the globe whirled by in darkness. The Suttons' child could not be found.

There was another way. "I shall be where you are, Jennifer Sutton, wherever that is." He drifted deeper, then slipped deeper still. Wherever you are. One, two, three. Now! But nothing happened. Seemingly, a lifetime of unrestricted soul travel, beginning in early childhood, had come to an end. Seemingly, also, all of Ted Willis' teaching had been a waste of time. Barnard now felt fear and anger about the likely loss of a gift for which he had long ago lost all appreciation.

But, even now, there was still another way. "I shall be where you are, Jennifer Sutton," he repeated. Intense concentration caused rapid surfacing from the trance. He forced it further. Thirty impulses per second . . . thirty-five . . . forty, and he pushed it further still — higher and higher up the scale, heartbeat racing, temples throbbing. Then, he could no longer ignore the fearsome delusions this state of mind had brought. He drifted back. To push higher up the scale was known to potentially bring death. It would be an irresponsible act.

A Power Without Name needed no hands to seize him. Held in a vice-like grip, unable to move, he was locked away in a place, too dark, too wet, too cold and too small to allow him to survive. Barnard had been forcibly thrust into the long-dead body of the child he'd been searching for. Despite his struggling, he was held as if forever, spirit and soul retching with the taste and smell of the corpse.

Release seemed to take an eternity. He knew only seconds had elapsed. Although no one noticed, the taste and smell would "stay" with him for days. The shocking memory of the event would not fade for many years. For once, the psychic healer had pushed the envelope too far.

The Spirit Guardians had surely witnessed what had happened to the mortal rookie of their platoon. Their deep concern could be felt. They did not know, however, who or what had caused the sudden, violent interment in a place already occupied.

"Christ! You could have killed me!" he cried. He was blaming all of them.

"Insubordinate you are!" came the response.

"I'll not do that again," he promised. "Not ever!"

"You are told so many times," was the answer.

"I didn't understand! I hate that feeling of not caring!" he cried out to the Guardians. "Why don't you make clear to me what's going on? Stop treating me like I was the platoon's bloody mascot. Jesus! Write it down and shove it in the bloody mail."

"None so defiant as he who challenges the Master Himself," was the suggestion.

"I didn't defy anyone. I didn't challenge anyone," the mortal argued. Suddenly he realized their comment concerned his swearing. "I always bargain with a little insistence. Even when I pray." There seemed to be no argument from the Spirit Guides on that particular score. George realized that even he did not agree with some of the claims he was making. "Okay, I come on a bit too heavy," he admitted.

"No braver fool in the universes," he was told.

"I'm sorry I fouled up. But that was an overkill, doing that to me," he accused them, still, when it was clearly not their doing.

"No greater dreamer on the planet," was the scathing remark.

The experience had brought George Barnard close to losing all reason and emotional control. He still felt he was walking a tightrope, badly balanced, teetering halfway between tranquillity and insanity. Feeling unable to go forward, incapable of stepping back, he pleaded with the Guardians, "I've had a bad, bad day, you Guys. Give me something important to do, something urgent, please." He was begging them for ongoing cooperation, fearful of their deserting him. "Save my dented ego."

"Sleep. We guide you," came the advice.

He took a long shower, scrubbed his skin until it was bright pink, and he rinsed his mouth many times. Even then, there seemed to be an all-pervading stench about him. But he remained defiant, rebellious and in partial denial of having caused the problem. "Who decides what's meant to be?" he grunted angrily. "Stuff the system for taking Jennifer. Bring her back!"

Minutes later, his head on the pillow, he thought of how he had misplaced her name. He thought of his racking his brain to recall the name he could have repeated a thousand times in his sleep. Of his thinking; What was the name of the Sutton child again?

"You knew she was gone, Barnard, you fool. You did not want to know," he grunted. Then he drifted off into a restless sleep.

The attempted healing of Jennifer Sutton followed countless successful ones over a period of many years. They all went smoothly, the mostly positive results and enviably high strike rates being their own rewards. Never before, but for knowing the Suttons really well, had Barnard been so insistent. Never before had he received punishment so severe—punishment of any kind. It shattered his confidence and lowered his pride to an all-time depth of depression.

In retrospect, pride must have been his problem. At the rate he was "bouncing around" the universe, there might have been a danger of his wanting to take over the running of it, sometime, sooner or later. And if this sounds like a confession, it probably is.

Little Miss Sutton had left her earthly home for good around ten o'clock, just an hour after Brian Sutton checked on the performance of the straightened drive-shaft—a little more than thirteen hours after Barnard's first attempted healing.

The healer strongly proposes that the very soul of the child had already been spirited away at that time. Her cast-off shell was still breathing . . . just a little longer.

A simple accident of time in an imperfect evolutionary world?

He doesn't really know.

11

"Get Off The Road!"

At the time George Mathieu Barnard first met the Spirit Guardian, ABC-22, the mortal was more than a little skeptical about the reality of the clearly spoken, as well as the mind-to-mind, information he received. Although in a deep trance, Barnard was distrustful of the fearsome looking Warrior, doubtful about the veracity of the answers he was getting from the Guardian. He was also quite convinced the Spirit Entity was nothing more than the lost Soul Self of a mortal who had lived long ago—a mere ghost, basically.

"So, what did you do for a living?" Barnard inquired.

"I am Warrior. I am Chief. I am Shaman. I am Teacher," came the Guardian's reply. The Spirit Entity seemed to want to make it clear he was hardly a part of history, but very much alive, although quite ancient.

All those professions, the rookie thought? Fat chance! At, say, thirty years of age? That must have been an all-time rapid rise to power.

It would take some years of association for the critical Barnard to learn to always take the Guardian seriously, to trust his own psychic ability, and to not ever judge his conclusions as they might well result from his imagination.

"Did you always act in a morally correct way?" the mortal asked at the time.

It was clear ABC-22 was not too impressed, but presently hardly distressed, about his actions of long ago—"during a time when there was no Law." The Guardian's recent excellent behavior, so ABC-22 claimed, "is vouched for by my Seraphic Superiors." His accidental trespasses of the past had long since been forgiven. But then the Spirit Guide followed up with what seemed like a lengthy confession of minor errors of the past, which Barnard failed to understand.

Only one aspect of this "confession" came through crystal clear. It was the mind-to-mind, full-color picture of a six-foot-high bush with shiny, healthy ovoid-shaped leaves. Many years later, George Mathieu considered having recognized that thought-transferred picture of the bush as being Khat, a hallucinogenic, still in common use in some African countries. Much later still he learned that it might have been a reference to the tree of life.

ABC-22, it became clear, was capable of easily traversing a great number of time facets, even of turning up in human dimensions of time and perhaps partaking of the mind-altering Khat.

How honest, how straight is this Spirit Guardian, Barnard thought? Things were becoming clearer now. His kind might have once given rise to the myth of incubi and succubi, George Mathieu considered. But he would never again risk hurting the Guardian's feelings by inquiring about such sordid behavior in ancient times. Barnard was convinced, however, that he would get a concise answer from the Warrior if he did bother to ask.

Despite his admiration for the Guardian's honesty about possible unethical conduct of so long ago, the mortal was still unwilling to admit any fault about his own stubborn attempt to heal Jennifer Sutton, despite his having been ordered by ABC-22 to leave Jennifer alone.

The Jennifer Sutton "disaster" was taking its toll. Barnard tried to analyze the deep depression that had so swiftly shrouded his mind in gloom. A downer of this intensity and duration did not at all fit with his psychological profile. He tended to shake off the inevitable setbacks rather efficiently.

George Mathieu had failed to heal the child, but the therapist had failed before. He had lost neighbors, family and friends before, and then he had recovered to go on with life, optimistically, full speed ahead. This depression could hardly be a simple psychological aberration. This had to be purely psychic, deeply spiritual, the therapist felt. The forced interment seemed to have crushed his very soul and nothing would lift his spirits.

The factory could flaming-well run itself, he decided. If not, they could close down the place and all go home. Barnard no longer cared. "Sort it out for yourself," he snapped on the telephone at the persistent Kevin Weiss. "I'm sick and depressed and I may even be enjoying my misery. It's all up to you now. Don't ring me again."

Occasionally, it seemed Barnard was taking his feet for a walk, wandering aimlessly around the grounds. Most of his days were spent on his swimming-pool patio with an ample supply of cigarettes and too many cups of coffee, doing nothing, and with nothing to do, feeling fatigued on awakening, exhausted by day's end.

Triggering an altered state of consciousness had become an unattainable goal.

He believed he had been deserted. And it hurt.

During this most difficult time, a small, pure white pigeon became his constant companion. Descending onto the swimming pool fence each morning, but remaining just out of George's reach, the bird faced him all day. Not until the sun was setting did it fly away, its powerful little wings loudly pounding the air as it took off. This had to be a strong, healthy pigeon.

There was no great secret about where it came from. It was the only white specimen belonging to a flock of perhaps eighteen birds. They hailed from a farm, miles away, but they occasionally scavenged for seed spilled from George's birdfeeder. How it could sit there all day, without food, without water, without feeling the need to join the rest of the flock, was a mystery to Barnard. The other birds frequently foraged in the grass below, but never bothered to join their diligent little white friend on the fence.

Is it sent to be with me, he wondered? A Peace Dove? I will never know, he thought. The mortal was unable to communicate with the Spirit Guardians. Psychically, Barnard was dead.

"Thank you for the thought," he told them just in case, "I think. But what shall I do for you in return? Give me something I can do." Daily, George Mathieu lived in fear of his having been dishonorably discharged from his platoon.

He was certainly temporarily expelled.

Slowly, his "psychic wounds" began to heal. The pigeon was gone and would not return. Barnard had become a little more active. However, the way he was, returning to, or even visiting his factory would serve no useful purpose. It was much too soon. He would likely upset more people, not just Kevin Weiss. He would stay at home for a little longer. He would repair his wooden paling fence, even if it took him days to do it. A crowbar, pliers, some nails and a hammer, he thought. All of it is in the garden shed. At last, he had had enough of his inaction. He stood and turned to gather the tools and nails.

"There's a snake there!" came a loud voice. He turned to see who might have spoken to him. Someone had blasted the information straight down his ear-hole. But there was nobody to be seen. "Thanks for the warning," he doubtfully mumbled.

"Like a damned fool, I always still look around," he grunted. The warning had been so resounding, so urgent. Moments later, it was still ringing in his right ear. Maybe I haven't been deserted, he thought. Maybe the deserter is I.

"Keep your eyes peeled, Barnard," he told himself as he slowly approached his garden shed. And there it was, hidden in the grass, a juvenile Brown Snake. Right, smack in the middle of the doorway was one of the most lethal serpents rearing its tiny head, ready to strike as George slowly approached. Where it lay, he would have stepped right on top of it in his bare feet. The snake would have struck him, nothing surer. That would have permanently solved my depression, he contemplated with some degree of morbid humor.

Barnard stood his ground at a safe distance and finally the snake slithered away. It was the first reptile of its kind he had seen on the property in fifteen years. It was also the last of its kind, an unusually long way from its regular habitat.

"Thank you," he told the Spirit Guardians. "You saved my life and that's for sure."

Someone is getting through to me, he mused. Even if I have become useless in communicating with them.

Immediately, that urgent need to be involved with the Guardians" projects surfaced again in his mind. "But what shall I do for you in return?" he asked. The thought of his no longer being an asset to them, but a permanent liability instead, bothered him greatly. To have things back the way they had been, was becoming an obsession, and he knew it. But a keen, professional understanding of an obsession will not make it go away.

Barnard had not been treating any of his patients for more than a week. That was fine. There were no urgent cases. Fixing the fence in the glaring sun put some urgently needed color back in his face. But he had to front up to his staff after the weekend, not a day later.

"So, I took a flippin' holiday. So what?" he practiced giving them his abrasive excuse.

The traffic was becoming more congested and George Mathieu eased off on the accelerator of the big company car. A quick glance in the rear-vision mirror showed a sleek, dark green sports car overtaking a line of vehicles with nowhere to go but to slam into oncoming traffic. "The joy of two-lane highways," Barnard muttered to no one in particular. His V8 leaped ahead. It braked just in time, only inches from the bumper in front, as the green hatchback gratefully darted into an urgently provided space behind the V8.

"That's one of his nine lives he owes me. Eight to go for this young cat. Will he grow up in time?" Barnard questioned aloud.

The little green monster was again edging over the double white line, as its driver seemed eager to pull out again. Quickly it darted back into its safe little slot behind Barnard's car as oncoming traffic whizzed by.

"He learned nothing!" Barnard remarked.

It had become a habit of his to make such statements in private. There had always been some Spirit Guardian to talk to. And if not, a Seraph or two would be around.

Don't ever count on getting answers to the mundane, he thought.

"That young fellow will get to his destination two minutes earlier, perhaps, if he gets there at all," George carried on with even more acrimony in his voice, "and if he does, he'll waste the next fifteen minutes telling everybody about his flaming excellent driving skills."

"Get off the road," an unknown voice casually sounded through his car.

"I'm going back to work! At last." Barnard objected, looking around to see who might have made that dumb remark. He smiled and added, "It's bloody Monday, if you didn't know."

"Get off the road! Now!" the voice commanded, loudly, urgently. A split-second vision of a multiple collision accompanied the insistent voice.

Barnard twisted his vehicle out of the lane of fast traffic and skidded to a halt on the wide gravel shoulder, some eighty meters from an intersection.

"Jeez," he gasped, "my car was in the middle of that. I saw that!" He pulled at the handbrake. "Who said that to me?" he asked, but there was no answer.

He switched off the engine, without knowing why, still dumbfounded about his having taken orders from an unknown voice. "I should have stayed at home. I'm still not feeling the best. Okay, I'll take another day off, if you think . . ."

"Oh, no!" he cried, as one after another the cars piled themselves up at the intersection. "Please don't let this be real," he prayed. Unable to stop in time, a tipper truck loaded high with organic fertilizer forced its way into the center of the crumpled pile-up. "Oh, shit!" Barnard cried.

The brand-new hatchback was in the middle of it all. It stood tipped-up on its nose, its twisted exhaust pipe pointing at the southeastern horizon.

"No one had better die in this shambles," Barnard insisted, as he raced up the hill. "Whoever you are, you saved my car!" He had to think about that some more. "Gosh! My life as well, I'd say. What for? Who am I then? What shall I do for you in return?"

The intersection looked like a well-stocked wrecker's yard with lots of lookers and no buyers.

"You look a bloody mess, George," Kevin Weiss suggested.

"That's just the kind of welcome back I expected from you," Barnard told him. Things will quickly return to normal, he thought. As normal as they get in this place.

"What happened to you?" Kevin was pulling up his nose at his boss. "You're covered in red paint!"

"There was a pile-up at the ring-road 3 intersection and some kid in a sports job cut an artery in his leg on something sharp and pointy. Blood squirting all over the place! I pressed my thumbs on it until the ambulance people arrived. There was really nothing else for me to do. Those are the delights that come your way, Kevin, old boy, when you've completed all your courses in physiology."

"Phew," said Weiss. "You may have saved his life."

"I'm damned sure of it. I think I saved his twice this morning," Barnard answered.

"He could pay you back by giving you Aids or something else deadly. Jeez! You'd better get out of those duds and into the shower, George. You've got it on your face and all."

"I've had worse than this all over me," Barnard answered flippantly. He was thinking of little Jennifer.

"I don't wanna know about that," the production man stated emphatically.

George Mathieu looked at him long and hard. "Good! No, you wouldn't want to know about that, Kevin," he assured Weiss.

Barnard meticulously scrubbed himself clean of the young driver's blood, but his thoughts were once again with the Jennifer Sutton interment.

In the days following, George Mathieu finally began to clearly wake up to the fact that if anyone had deserted anyone, it was he who had willfully abandoned his Spirit Guardians by trying to go it alone in the Jennifer Sutton case. He was expelled from his platoon, maybe for good. The Guardians were still about, however, watching over him.

But in all fairness, the presence of that little white pigeon could just have been a random, though extremely unusual occurrence. The timely caution about the snake's presence could not be questioned and neither was there any doubt about the advance warning of the sudden carnage on ring-road 3.

The emotionally distraught rookie was out of touch with his Superiors. Lines of communication were cut, but only one way.

Spare a thought for these long-lived Teachers of the Halfway Realm. No sooner have they taught their mortal associates the very basics of Universe Communication, than their marginally intelligent pet mammals have reached their in-use expiration dates. And again, the Spirit Guardians must go and search out new recruits, teaching, lecturing and tutoring their new novices all over again.

Contact with humans is hard to establish, not in the least because the vertebrates are almost always entirely inept in perceiving the Guardians' mind-to-mind communications. Once established, contact can be so easily lost. But the Eleven-Eleven of the Halfway Realm never give up on anyone they adopt.

What great affection they must feel for their thankless, thoughtless, distant planetary cousins of flesh and blood!

Spare a thought.

Evolution's Aspiration

After each fall
  he stands and moves on,
  his resolutions come to naught,
  until he ultimately takes decisive action.

Then triumph never tasted so sweet,
  as it does following failure since failure.

But his rich rewards remain without value,
  until they are shared with all,
  and slake the thirst of evolution's true aspiration.

Each time again there is progress, slow,
  in achieving the true resolve of time/space life.

As he charts the wide oceans of knowledge,
  he sees his cup of wisdom shrink and shrink.

He is an evolutionary animal,
  urged along the burdensome road to perfection,
  drinking from but a thimble, still.

part five

The "Re-enlistment"

Typical of the response of a mere mortal, Barnard saw the Jennifer Sutton interment as punishment meted out to him because of his insubordination. To his mind, the Spirit Guardians further disciplined him by cutting off all communications, and for many weeks he felt like a minor, expelled from school for serious misbehavior. The Guardians might not ever want him back in their platoon, he feared. In reality, something quite unknown to the Guardians had gone wrong. It was little more than an unexpected hiccup of some unknown Force in an imperfect evolutionary world.

Barnard would not gain that necessary insight until much later.

True to their function as tireless Teachers, the Spirit Guardians set about educating their rookie in a fashion that would make him understand what had happened before. They did so in a profound and unexpected way. But even then, the slow-on-the-uptake human again missed the point.

The inexhaustible Guardians made yet a second attempt to get through to him. And this time the penny dropped. Barnard now fully appreciated some of the perplexing aspects of one of the most complex creatures inhabiting the universe—evolutionary humans.

12

Virginia Jamieson

Shortly after his induction into the platoon, a much younger Barnard came up with a hare-brained notion. He thought he might try to slip into the Halfway Realm and, with the Guardians' assistance, actually stay there. It seemed like such a good idea at the time to become invisible at will, never to feel hunger, or become sleepy. Above all, it seemed most profitable to be able to remember everything and live forever, just like his Spirit Companions did.

For one who was constantly seeking knowledge for its own sake, a flawless, "photographic" memory would be worth more than all his worldly possessions, even with his firm's check account thrown in. He earnestly approached the Guardians to obtain their help in carrying out the nutty plan.

At the time, Barnard had been squeezed through the wringer of life, backwards, sideways and doubled up. He was still licking his wounds months after the event. But with only a vague show of compassion, the mortal was told his dumb proposal was off the menu.

ABC-22's somewhat condescending rebuttal, "You are human! You cannot be like us", made Barnard wonder if Spirit Guardians were endowed with real emotions, even a sense of humor. Who would even dream of wanting to permanently enter their timeframe if there weren't an occasional good laugh to be had? Theirs would be a sad, sad lot. In the years of celestial-mortal cooperation that followed, Barnard learned they did have emotions and a great sense of the ludicrous.

But many weeks after the shocking Jennifer Sutton interment, it was George Mathieu who seemed to have permanently misplaced his sense of humor. He felt isolated, and was missing his best friends. Then, they made him experience something he could not have foreseen in his wildest dreams.

It happened in an immeasurably small fraction of time. Drifting off to sleep one moment, the rookie found himself standing on a concrete pier in the very next instant. There was hardly a hint of color in all he saw—the dark but tranquil bay, the somber, misty night-sky, the concrete pier with its steel safety railing. To his left a distant modern city, at his right, some eight paces away, stood the noble Warrior. Behind ABC-22 stood a group of some ten, perhaps twelve entities of widely varied sizes.

Barnard wondered why they were so difficult to discern, but he marveled at their vastly different sizes. "You brought many friends, Bzutu," the human remarked, "a crowd. But they're hard to see and so are you."

Something was different about this trip, but the mortal did not know what it was. He had seen other entities before; though never so many at the one time and never before had they looked so vague.

There was no answer from the Warrior. No introductions. ABC-22 shifted his weight, observing his mortal student patiently at all times.

"This is not one of my lucid dreams, is it?" Barnard asked.

"We are here," came the Guardian's reassuring answer.

"You said you would guide me," the human reminded him. "I asked for something worthwhile to do to make up for my willful behavior. I asked for something important to do, so you know I can be trusted again. This can't be it! Are you playing a joke on me?"

"This is it," came the somewhat loud and abrasive response.

Barnard looked around. There was nothing to do on this cold, wet and lonely pier but a spot of fishing. What a stupid idea to come here at night, he thought.

"Get about your task, then!" ABC-22 sounded somewhat impatient. He sounded like his student should already know all of what needed to be done.

Barnard looked back at the gentle swell of the bay. There was nothing much to see. Only a solitary seagull circled in the mist and semi-darkness, perhaps fifty meters away, hovering now, circling anti-clockwise, and hovering again.

Something came to mind. "A sentinel marking a target?" the rookie asked. "Ah! Is there a school of fish down there?" he wanted to know, but no one answered. "We never brought our fishing rods, nets, or scuba gear."

He was quickly convincing himself the entire effort was meant to be a joke. "Somebody might inform that bird it's jolly night-time now," he suggested. He laughed and looked at the group. None of those present appeared to share the mortal's feelings for making fun. They were a solemn looking lot. Barnard didn't mind about how they felt and shouted at the bird, "Eh! Feathers! Go home! Time to go to sleep!"

Then he looked down. There was indeed something in the water, right below the hovering bird. As if on cue with his realizing this, the gull drifted away.

It was hard to make out what this object might be. Mostly submerged, the lapping swell momentarily pushed it into view, then out of sight again for many long seconds.

What could it be, he wondered? A dead pig? "You all brought me out here for a dead pig?" He felt deeply insulted. "That is *so* unkind."

"Get it now," ABC-22 ordered.

The human hesitated, unwilling to touch the pig, and afraid to disobey his Superior, he stayed planted on the spot. "I think I'll go home now," he suggested meekly. "Better that I go home, you Guys."

"Get it now!" ABC-22 insisted in the gruffest of voices.

Entirely guided by those on the pier, it seemed, Barnard hovered out with ease, grabbed a limb and slowly dragged the dead body back to the pier. He marveled at his own strength and fitness as he clambered back up onto the pier, lifting the bloated, heavy load from the dark waters with notable ease.

Still feeling belittled and disgraced, he unceremoniously slammed his morbid catch against the steel safety rail. He stepped back and viewed the distasteful blob of a creature. "Oh, my God! It's a woman!" he cried out.

She moved ever so slightly, and without a moment's thought Barnard dropped to his knees beside her, pinning her shoulder against the railing. But she would not open her eyes and the mortal knew he would sense nothing from her closed eyes.

"Spit it out!" he suddenly urged her. That message had seemingly come from nowhere. That was inspired, for sure, he concluded. That came from all those entities over there. "Spit it out! All of it, woman!" he urged her on. It seemed to be the right thing to say to her.

A small stream of water shot from her mouth. "All of it! All of it! Now!" Barnard kept urging her, shaking her by the shoulder.

Suddenly, a great stream of water gushed a distance of some meters and the fat and bloated body of a woman, formerly seemingly overweight and scarcely recognizable as human, turned into that of a slim young lady. As she took on her appropriate shape, so did many bruises on her body become evident. Her skin toned up somewhat and there was a deep slash mark across her throat. She felt so very cold.

All the mortal's inhibitions seemed to be left behind in another world, another reality. He felt only tenderness and charity towards this poor, naked little victim. Above all, there was a pressing urgency for him to get her to liven up.

"Spit it all out, girl!" he told her again. But there was nothing more to spit out. "Look at me now! Look at me!" he insisted. Her head had lolled forward like that of a well-worn rag doll. "Open your eyes, lass! Look at me!"

Slowly, she raised her head like a fearful, cowering dog. She was breathing, unaware of there being no need for her to breathe.

"I'm George Mathieu Barnard. And you are now free," he informed her. They are not my words, he thought! They were not even my thoughts! "Who put that in my mind?" he grunted, but there was no answer.

Their eyes met at last and all the young woman's emotions became his. He sensed the horror she had suffered long ago, and all of her fears. He felt the love she had given to many in her short life, the bitter lessons learned by her. Her hopes and plans. Her needs and wants. Her slow progress in another time. All of her emotions became those of the Guardians' understudy, but he could not gather a single fact.

"Who did this to you?" he sharply demanded to know. "Who killed you?"

With that question she whisked away, upwards and at great speed. Barnard was left kneeling on the concrete pier, looking at his empty hand, which only a moment before had held her shoulder to give her support.

"Wow! She flies faster than anybody can!" He stood and turned to all assembled. There was great admiration in his voice. "Can she ever hike! Brilliant!" He felt so excited. Then doubts entered his mind and he turned back to the Guardian. "Bzutu, this was not a lucid dream, eh?" he asked.

"It is not. And we are here," his Superior answered.

"This was urgent and important, like you promised me?" George asked.

"It is so. Go home, George Mathieu. It is done," said the Guide.

Barnard noticed the other Entities were seemingly fading into thin air. But ABC-22 was still by his side. I can't leave now! Leaving now would be very wrong, the mortal thought.

"Go home. It is done," the Guide told him again. "What takes you so long? Go home. Time to go to sleep."

"Not likely," the belligerent mortal answered. He stood fast and held onto the railing. "I don't even know her name," he complained. "All her emotions became mine. We were so close; we were as one. I must know her name to find her again, later." A powerful bond had been formed, so quickly, and the mortal was concerned about never meeting her again.

Although all the other entities were now invisible to him, Barnard sensed they were still there. And he sensed their disbelief of the abject contempt for authority of such a willful human.

"I'll wait here till the cows come home," the rookie promised the Guardian, "you know me, Bzutu." Barnard squeezed the cold railing for dear life. "I must know her name."

Tempers were rising. Barnard could feel it. It bothered him greatly not to be able to see the other Entities to gauge their feelings more clearly. But the Warrior was in charge, no doubt of that, and he was visibly embarrassed by the student's tenacity.

"So stubborn you are," the Warrior complained.

At last it showed, as in bright sunshine—a flat, yellow wooden arrow pointing due west. Attached to a square wooden post, its deeply routed black lettering read VIRGINIA ST.

"Fine," the human mumbled. "Virginia it is. Might she have been so fortunate as to have inherited a surname as well?" he asked. "Yes?"

Quickly it appeared. A round-edged and enameled metal plate with raised white letters on a dark blue ground. Stuck to a building and facing south, JAMISON Ave.

"Virginia Jamison?" he queried. "Oh, I see. Put an E in there. Virginia Jamieson!" He was delighted to know her name. "Gosh, what took you so long?" he asked jokingly.

"Will you go home now?" came the loud, blunt request.

"Where are we then?" he asked in turn. The answer came, but he missed it in part. It sounded like, "frisco."

Many summers of diving on the coral reefs, it seemed, had affected his hearing in everyday mortal existence. Coral deafness, apparently, is just as troublesome in the Halfway Realm, he mused. "What's a frisco?" he asked. A mental picture of an ice-cream cone danced before his eyes. Vanilla flavored, George presumed. Ridiculous! "You're messing with my mind," he reproached the now smiling Guardian.

"San Francisco!" the Warrior informed him.

"You *were* messing with my mind, Bzutu," Barnard accused him. "You do it all too often. I know you do." He stopped to think about being so far from home and he glanced back at the mist-shrouded city. It suddenly looked so different, so old. "What's the use of my being all the way out here?" he asked. "I belong in Australia. There are thousands and thousands of psychics in this big land who could set the lass' soul free. Why did you transport me all this way?"

"Your request," sounded the immediate response. "Urgent and important. You are not a Specialist. You come to learn many things, very fast. Go home now! So persistent you are."

The mortal gripped the railing more tightly still. He glanced back at the city. 1903? 1908? Ah! 1911! Prohibition! "It's long ago, but someone now knows this

Jane Doe's name," he muttered. "That is San Francisco! No, it isn't. It was!"

The Jamieson girl's soul must have been listed for urgent release, he thought. "Why and how did she die, Bzutu?" he asked. "It seems such a waste. She really wasn't much more than a child, this one."

The rookie had pushed the Guardian too far. The Warrior's patience had entirely run out. The rail Barnard had clasped suddenly ceased to exist. He was now observing a smartly dressed Virginia Jamieson, being kicked and punched around in an upstairs room. She was roughly tossed into a wide, deep chair. Then, while she was held by the hair, and from behind, a small sharp knife cut her throat. She passed out but she stubbornly refused to die.

Next up, the boot of a black, vintage model car opened up. It was parked in a deserted street in the industrial quarter, the lower part of the town. Rain was bucketing down on the city and streetlights were few. Four eager hands removed a heavy, round and patterned manhole cover and the same four eager hands took a rug from the boot of the vehicle.

Head first, Virginia Jamieson's naked body slipped from the rug and splashed into the raging storm water torrent below. Somehow robbed of all conscious fear, and just before the iron cover slammed back into place, Barnard slipped in after her. She struggled weakly, then washed away.

"You didn't bleed to death, Miss," he told her unemotionally. "You . . . actually drowned." He was coldly, casually informing her of the precise circumstances of her demise.

He followed the body through the lengthy cavern. One of the rusty bars was missing from the grille at the end of the tunnel. Unaware of the fact she was now quite dead, Virginia Jamieson's sleek little body slipped through the gap and washed into the bay. Barnard climbed back onto the pier. He was back in the precise spot he had started from. "So, *that's* how it was," he remarked, expecting to be told to urgently head for home. But no one had waited for him to return. He was alone.

At least, so it seemed.

In a mere moment in time he was back in his room, sitting on the edge of his bed and wondering why he could feel so good, so suddenly, and after such a troubling experience. Less than fifteen minutes had elapsed since he had closed his eyes to enjoy a night of undisturbed sleep, just before the Guardians spirited him away. This is what he had asked for many long years ago, only to be told he was not allowed to share their timeframe. "You did it!" he told the Guardians. "That was great!"

He was wide awake now, feeling pleased. Weeks of bother and depression caused by the Jennifer Sutton interment had been taken from his mind, so quickly. Again, he had given ABC-22 a hard time, but there were things Barnard needed to know.

Had not the Warrior told him, "You came to learn many things very fast?" Barnard mumbled sarcastically, "Not a Specialist. So persistent you are George Mathieu. Yes, a damned-hard-to-get-along-with nuisance, Bzutu, or I'd never learn a thing."

The Guardians must understand why their student is so obstinate, he thought. They would know more about me than I do.

The Essence, Soul, or Astral Self of Virginia Jamieson had been dormant, resting in "Frisco" bay for a long time. A diminished personality, but all the emotions of experiential living were contained in the "ethereal package" that had now been set free. An awareness of self, and a realization of the passing of time, had surely been missing. That much, at least, was obvious to Barnard.

She might have been what some call a ghost—an accident of disorderly dissolution of the component parts of a highly complex human creature. How this long-forgotten aspect of the young woman could take off, seemingly unassisted, was a mystery to him.

More of a mystery was the pathetic, self-satisfied feeling now marinating his soul. His ledger, he felt, was again completely in the black. Barnard was truly delighted the debt had been discharged in full. A debt to Whom, he wondered? About that he had no idea. There were still so many questions.

13

The Hermit

Caring for his family, operating a manufacturing plant, and running a part-time clinic can be tough if you want to do a reasonable job. If you want to make an individual success of all three, it'll have you spinning like a top. But this was a Tuesday, a workday on which George Barnard did little more than leisurely drive himself across town. He needed to seek out one of the greatest minds he ever knew—a mind belonging to a quaint old man who hated chlorinated water, computers, airplanes, and unannounced visitors.

And this old man wouldn't own a telephone if you sent him one for Christmas, and so, his visitors all came unannounced.

Barnard needed answers. There were questions on his mind, still.

A huge bougainvillea with large sprays of magenta flowers had almost entirely swallowed up Professor Dr. Edward Willis' sizeable cottage. Some years ago, George remembered, it had already demolished part of the guttering and a down pipe. It was really flourishing now, lifting many of the terracotta roof tiles of his former lecturer's home.

Willis had shrunk somewhat in height, it seemed, and his thinning hair, moustache and beard were now the snowiest of snowy white. Slowed down by age, it took him some time to open his door. He seemed neither pleased nor displeased about his student of long ago visiting him, but his handshake was warm.

"I tried to call you on the phone," George joked, "You must have been out."

"There's nothing more I can, or want to teach you, Barnard," Willis suggested bluntly. "You might as well go home now." All the same, he opened his door wide and led the therapist into a living room where all available wall space was now occupied with loaded-up bookshelves. Ted Willis had turned his home into a veritable firetrap.

"Did you bring your own poison?" he asked. His dislike for Barnard's treasured stimulant would always remain.

"If you can provide the hot water," Barnard suggested, "there's enough coffee and sugar right here in this bag to keep us both on a high all day."

"I would never sink so low as to push those kinds of drugs onto a friend," Willis chided him. "But it's your life. Shorten it, why don't you. Do with it as you see fit."

Willis was probably born with that attitude. He would never change. But he did listen that morning with closed eyes and wrinkled brow as George Mathieu recounted in detail the Sutton and Jamieson experiences. The host was thoughtful, seemingly cautious in his response.

"I have a distant relative," Willis began, "and in his younger years, he used to go into disused mine tunnels. He used to reclaim the stays that propped up the ceilings and stopped the mines from caving in. Those heavy wooden props were worth a few shillings, but he could never take them all. That would have been much too dangerous. One day he got greedy—he claims unlucky—and the whole shebang caved in on him. He took one prop too many and it took two days of careful digging to free him. He lived to talk about it. But the jury is still out on the matter. Did he, during those years, take greater and greater risks? Did familiarity breed contempt? Or is a mere human capable of knowing what dangers lurk in kilometers of overburden?"

The old lecturer opened his eyes and raised his bushy white eyebrows at the younger man. "You did the same thing, George." He waited and observed his ex-student closely. "You pulled one stunt too many and brought the ceiling down on yourself. And it took your Spirit Guide Buddies weeks to figure out how to dig you out of the mess you yourself created. You challenged a Force of which you have no knowledge. Did you say you thereafter asked to be given something urgent and important?" he asked slyly.

Barnard nodded. "And ABC-22 said it would be there when I was asleep," he answered. "But I waited and waited! Cripes! It took them five weeks."

Willis smiled. "A thousand-and-one inter-office memos in triplicate, passed all the way up the line to the Man Himself, and finally the method for extricating you from the debris was approved."

"I sure was in a mess," Barnard agreed.

Willis paused, vaguely grunting with mock sardonic pleasure about Barnard's weeks of unease. "What makes you think this universe isn't run like any other learning institution? You see your Tutor, who talks to your Lecturer, who goes to lobby the Department Head. On to Administration, Finance, the Bursar, for an estimate of the cost, to the Vice Chancellor and right to the top, the Chancellor. Don't I know it! And if you can't get your assessment ready in time because you can only work a few hours a day whilst lying on your stomach, what happens? The whole university ends up knowing you've got a whopping great boil the size of a golf-ball on your butt. They might all want to come and see it getting lanced. And there are all those entities you talked about, looking at you with your pants down."

Willis was enjoying himself. After the many years since he taught Barnard he remembered how the student had suffered with a boil in a most uncomfortable place.

"So, what was it that caved in on me?" Barnard asked, ignoring the remark about the boil.

"A Force, an Energy, a mind-endowed Power, capable of giving you what you insisted on. However, like the rest of this universe, it is still not evolved enough to know what you really wanted. Don't do it again! Don't do it just to prove you can do it. And if you push yourself to fifty cycles per second, it may well be the last thing you do. You landed yourself deeply into schizophrenia territory."

Momentarily, he became pensive. "I'm getting old, George, and right up until now, I would have happily gone to my grave, and under the mistaken impression I had at least taught *you* something useful. What a disastrous, total waste of a life it's been for me." There were lights dancing in his eyes. This was the Ted Willis that George Barnard had come to know so well.

Suddenly he remarked, "You must like that Sutton family a lot."

"I'm just a sucker for kiddies," George suggested. "Nothing serious, a minor aberration, it'll pass."

"Urgent and important," Willis mused aloud. "So, what was so urgent and important about releasing that useless astral self?" he asked. "That ghost, or whatever it was, of the Jamieson woman?"

Barnard shrugged. "Hard to say, Ted. I asked for something urgent and important. And ABC-22 never lets me down. He never will."

"Except for your own urgent healing needs, nothing else was either urgent or important," Willis stated bluntly.

"No way!" Barnard told him heatedly.

"Keep that metabolism down," Willis suggested. "I don't want any gory accidents on my carpet. But I agree with you entirely. There are two aspects of equal importance here. That great transference of emotion you felt in your soul, that was one. And for the Jamieson's astral remains it was a long-overdue confrontation with a fact.

Remember? You asked, "Who *killed* you?" You stated a fact and in so doing, you caused the sudden realization of that fact and the release."

He paused momentarily. "Basically you said, "You are dead, go fly away." But your soul was not a part of you when you followed her through that storm-water drain. You were without emotion when you told her she had drowned. Your Spirit Self took your conscious mind back in time and your soul kept clinging to that railing on the pier until you re-emerged in that very same spot. To, in part, re-assemble. To then make it home and fully reassemble." He paused and scowled at his ex-student. "You are now traversing so many realities of time. It would be a big help to you if you found out more about where you are in time when you get there. Also, ask them what aspects of yourself are present on those occasions."

"I should do that more often," Barnard agreed.

Again, the old psych lecturer paused. "Of all the psychology students . . . oh, and others I have taught how to meet up with their Spirit Guides, George, you are, I'm rather certain, the only one who is dealing with the Eleven-Eleven of the Halfway Realm. Your Spirit Friends are a special, a most powerful group, with codes instead of names. I fear you are most casual about your association with them, willful, obstinate, insistent, like you always were. You just don't realize what favor was bestowed upon you when you were accepted by those unique creatures."

Barnard nodded. "I agree," he finally admitted. "I give them a hard time. Had Louise and I not done that course with you, I would have probably never known who they were and joint projects would likely run more smoothly. I would still be wondering who was waking me up at precisely eleven minutes past eleven at night, although, I would presumably be acting on their urgings more intuitively. More successfully, I'd say."

"Very likely," Willis answered, "you would learn a lot less, also. They really are your Teachers. You just don't always catch on to what they're telling you. There is a subtle parallelism, as well as a delicate incongruity, between the two events, George."

"Like what?" Barnard inquired.

"You work it out," Willis answered. He suddenly decided to change the subject of the conversation. "That friend of many years you just mentioned, Louise Hewitt, is making a name for herself Down South," he remarked. "She opened her own clinic some years ago, but she will be in town three weeks from now." It was Willis' way of ending the discussion about the Sutton interment and the Jamieson release.

"I'd like to meet up with Lou Lou," Barnard suggested. "It has been a few years."

"I'll let her know and she can give you a call, George," Willis suggested. "She and I intend to hire a car to go to that weekend Psychology Convention in Tumut, and she's flying straight home when it's over."

"Really? I'm booked in there as well. You two had better come with me," Barnard offered. "We'll drive instead of flying there. You could call it a coincidence, Ted, my seeing you again when she happens to be coming around, and all three of us ending up in the same place."

"There's no such thing as a coincidence, George. There never was."

His childhood teachers generally disliked Master Edward Willis. The boy, an only child of middle-aged British migrants, was considered to be disruptive and a virtual non-producer. In fact, young Master Willis was bored with classroom routine since he received few answers to his probing, uninhibited, or what were often thought of as most scandalous, questions.

His parents worked in their family enterprise, and over many years, they amassed a great fortune. Their savings were regularly converted into bricks and mortar.

Slowly their investments grew into sizeable holdings, but neither parent cared to spend much time with their lone offspring and heir.

As a teenager, Ted learned to cook and care for himself. He enjoyed his own company, and studied a great variety of subjects. He never married, but was always at ease and charming in female company.

Not until his middle twenties, after years of wandering around India and Tibet, did he aim for a career in psychology. Not until his thirtieth year did he receive his very first paycheck as a qualified psychologist. Always, however, parapsychology was his number one interest, though he felt this branch of the science was getting nowhere fast.

Ted could read auras and people's moods and minds so well that he tended to use very few words in a one-to-one conversation. When lecturing, he tended to spot his fatigued and sleepy students the moment they dozed off. There was no place to hide in his crowded lecture rooms. He would wake them by loudly calling their names as he saw their auras change color.

Dowsing, psychometry and mind-to-mind communication were some of his main interests. He was also a regular and ardent firewalker. When pressed, he admitted Zen Buddhism would be his choice, if he were really forced to adopt just one religion. He had adopted none and respected all. Ted was a complex man and his life, also, became rather complex when his parents died within two years of each other.

He was wealthy now, but his existence remained frugal. With his minimum needs and few wants, other than more books and even more books, his fortune meant little to him. He never owned a car and only at age forty-eight obtained a drivers license. His great personal fortune, so suddenly inherited, also brought him instant headaches of tenants with leaking taps and broken flyscreens.

Tenants cramped his style.

When Barnard met Willis, the professor's holdings had long ago been formed into a Limited Company and Ted was one of its four directors. Apart from the dividends, which mostly came his way, Ted was entitled to a director's fee for attending regular meetings. But years prior, it had been agreed by all, that if he decided not to attend these meetings, the Company Limited would double his fees for his remaining at home, playing the hermit.

He was so disruptive.

Ted and Louise would arrive at the Barnards' homestead during the following Thursday afternoon to catch a few hours' sleep. They would depart just after midnight on the Friday morning and settle in for an extra night in Tumut. The weekend convention was to end early on the Sunday afternoon and they planned to immediately make their way home.

Louise would take a flight home from Canberra, her best connection. She was pushed for time and eager to get back to her husband, children, and her busy psychology practice, but she enjoyed Ted's company too much not to make the car trip. There was another reason for Louise to have come so far north and for her to want to be in Tumut outside of her eldest child's holiday time. Her older sister, Catherine, a long-time resident of the mountain town, would celebrate her fortieth birthday on that Friday. The sisters were close friends and this would become their celebration of the year.

Barnard didn't mind driving those long hours. He had made the trip many times. There would also be lots of lake trout on the menu. Delicious! Although his work was stacking up, he wanted to, most of all, spend the time with Ted, both at the convention and whilst driving there and back.

The brilliantly minded, eccentric Ted Willis, although an ardent astral traveler, would never fly in an airplane.

14

The German Nun

Barnard was well on his way back to his factory, and from visiting Willis when the professor's statements about similarity and difference finally became clear.

There sure was a parallelism between the Sutton and Jamieson events. Both dealt with some kind of aberration in the normal procedure of dying. Simple! That was easy to see. The incongruity was harder to pick up on, yet Barnard eventually worked it out.

Jennifer Sutton had still been breathing and yet the eternal Essence of her being had swiftly departed. Virginia Jamieson had drowned but her Soul Self had been unable to leave. It pointlessly stayed around. It was all so obvious now.

"I rather prefer to be a healer than a psychic undertaker," Barnard joked aloud. "It's so much better to keep body, mind, Spirit and soul together. And healthier."

He did not expect an answer to the obvious, but felt the Guardians might not care a great deal about throwaway physical bodies. "Why should you care?" he asked.

He would soon learn that this was not the case. Far from it.

Professor Willis, ancient as he was, had once more out-thought and out-reasoned his student of long ago. Willis was one of the best teachers George Mathieu had ever known. If the professor paid him a compliment, it really meant something.

Compliments were few and far between. But if Willis was "having a go," as it was called, one really smarted. For George it was a double dilemma to be in Willis' verbal firing line. The already older-than-average student still blushed like no other. That profuse blushing had been even worse in his high school days. "Poor me," he mumbled, remembering one of the worst embarrassments he ever suffered as a boy. "Actually, poor Jéjé! That strange nun was Jéjé's teacher, not mine." How fearful Jéjé had been of that sister Eugenie, he mused. Put that old woman out of your mind, Barnard, he thought. Work awaits.

But the memory, and seemingly even the nun's presence, would not leave him. The woman's "ghost" seemed to inhabit his workroom for the rest of the day.

Would this mental pre-occupation have something to do with Jehanne Colette, he wondered? There had been quite a few 11:11 courtesy wake-up calls. No, he thought, Jéjé is fine. That German nun, he considered?

That's ridiculous!

Jehanne Colette, mostly referred to as Jéjé, was George's only sister. Therefore, the attainment of favorite sister status was hardly a great achievement on her part, although the two were close. None of her brothers, except George Mathieu, resembled real people according to Jéjé's frequently expressed opinion.

One might almost suggest Jéjé to have been adopted into the family, just so the Barnards would have at least one girl. She was already so totally feminine, and out-of-place amongst the boys.

Gentle natured, she was an accomplished musician at age nine, and she began to fashion delightful dolls' clothes by age ten. But, one had to be careful with her feelings. She was so easily hurt. And Jéjé worried about lots of things to which no one else would ever give a second's thought.

George had long ago given in to holding Jéjé's hand, all the way to her girls' school. It was most embarrassing for the boy. He was, after all, already six years old! Somehow his sister needed that closeness, although she was always still peeved with him for his being a boy. It was likely that the silent, peaceful youngster remained the least threatening to her of all her brothers. Almost from the day of his birth, she had spent much time with the infant, chatting away for hours, and perhaps still hoping he would one day turn into a girl.

Jehanne Colette did not perceive her world as a safe place. For the greater part of her childhood German invaders had occupied her country. And, to her mind, anything German was bad. Now the greatest threat to Jéjé's happiness was Sister Eugenie, a German nun, who claimed the voice of the Good Lord could be heard inside everyone's head. All one had to do was listen. She was an imposing, forbidding presence, and George's sister was truly frightened of her.

Jéjé and little George would often hide behind the girls' school's privet hedge and spy on Sister Eugenie through the foliage. They would look at, and comment on, her furry moustache, her piercing eyes, her manly features, until the nun rang the school bell. Then they would both run to get to their classes in time, laughing all the way.

Sister Eugenie was really a nasty Emperor Penguin, Jéjé claimed. She was a black and white tent with an evil woman hiding inside it. She rapped her girls over the knuckles for just one Dutch word out of place, and that in a district where the ancient dialect changed about every five kilometers—going North, South, or East. George felt sorry for Jéjé, mostly for her being an only girl, but also for her having the villainous Sister Eugenie as a teacher for a whole year.

He had come to believe he was lucky to be a boy, and on his sister's say so alone. Also because he would never have the miserable Sister Eugenie as a teacher. Little did he know their paths would cross, more than once.

Their high school exams were brutally squeezed into two short days—sixteen subjects, no less. The English, Dutch, French, and German tests were split between written and verbal examinations, and that made it twenty exams all up. Too bad if you were not feeling too good. After three years of high school blood, sweat, and tears, that diploma was swinging on your performance on just those two short days. If it weren't actually legal, which it was, it would surely be criminal.

George was a healthy, but exhausted fourteen-year-old. He could have walked out on his last exam, German, verbal, and still held his position near the top of his class, even if he scored a big fat zero for ditching that last exam. He knew he had done really well, but German had remained the weakest of his languages. Thirty minutes of pressing his fatigued brain into action? Hell, why not? They would all be able to go home soon after that.

Someone found his name on the schedule. She pointed George to a table in the center of the big examination hall. And there she was, of all people: Sister Eugenie. Trust his flaming bad luck, the nun would be his examiner. It was surely one chance in a million. Already her all-seeing, forbidding eyes were on the young student.

Cautiously, gingerly, he approached her, and he politely greeted her in her native language. He greeted her co-examiner. There was no reply from either of them. That was unsettling. The young male examiner was lying back in his chair, eyes closed, his nose pointed at the ceiling. He was to take no part whatever in the conversation. That was wrong!

These two were both meant to keep the student on the go. That's what they were being paid to do. But the nun's sharp eyes were on George. She was looking right through him, silently, searching out his very soul. Fear pinned him to the ground, and right where he stood. If only the ground would swallow him up, forever. He so wished it would.

Sister Eugenie blinked a few times. Again, she looked at him intently. Gradually, that stern look changed to apprehensive wonderment, then repulsion, then fear, then utter distress, and finally panic. And George sensed her feelings as if they were his own. My God! That was spooky! Who did she think he was? She was scaring the daylights out of him. Poor Jéjé, he thought. Life, during one long year of putting up with that evil woman, must have been unbearable for that sweet girl who always still needed so much tender care.

If Sister Eugenie had leaped from her chair, right then, right there, and had run off down the hall screaming, George would not have been surprised. Coming face-to-face with Satan himself could not have distorted her face any more than it was. The woman was panic-stricken, and all her feelings were also his. There were no facts.

Suddenly, there was a glimmer of recognition on her face. She visibly relaxed, and as she did, so did George. He felt it. She looked pleased and intrigued, happy now. Excited. Warm feelings of affection came from her mind. And he shared these feelings with her. They were her feelings, sure enough, but they also, instantly, became those of George Mathieu. Sister Eugenie had put his emotions on a giant seesaw, and the woman was scaring him half to death.

She stood and walked around the table. Larger than life, it seemed, she faced the young man. And then she hugged him. Him! George Barnard! That often blushing, shy, fourteen-year-old boy! Right there, smack in the middle of an examination hall full of people, he was being hugged, almost smothered, by the nun so many children feared.

He knew he was blushing. Red as a beet he would be. Looking over his right shoulder at the crowd. No one was watching them. Thank Christ! He would never tell anyone of this till the day he died. If someone glanced up at him, he would deny it ever happened, or he would leave home for a distant shore.

And then, suddenly, she held him by the shoulders and at arm's length. Pleased with him and proud of him, as if he was her long-lost relative, she was looking him up and down. So genuinely happy to see him, it seemed. She hugged him again. Fearful of her affection, he froze, blushing, praying she would let go of him. Looking over his left shoulder now, he noticed not a soul was looking in their direction. What a blessing! Thank the Dear Lord for small mercies!

Finally, she let go of him, and calmly pointed to his chair. The examination was about to begin. But he stammered and stuttered. His mind was a blank. Sister Eugenie, for all the genuine affection her soul contained, had destroyed every ounce of his self-confidence.

He had studied up on the German composers, their education system, their import/export figures, and much more, hoping to lead the conversation in that direction, and control it. It was all gone! Lost from his mind. Her crazy actions had ruined his memory, devastated his emotions, and racked his feeble little mortal mind.

The nun stuck with him. That encouraging smile never left her face. She was urging him on. Helping him along, making suggestions, calmly, systematically. Then it happened.

That German verbal examination, despite some ten minutes of wasted time, became the example of what a verbal exam should be like; rapid-fire communication. He would have never believed himself to be capable of it. There was no higher mark on his high school diploma than his score of that short session. And there was more.

During the few remaining weeks of schooling left to complete after the examination days, he surprised everyone, including his teachers and himself, with what had happened to his command of that language. A quantum leap of progress had been made. As well, Sister Eugenie's mild, though distinct, Bavarian accent was an unshake-able part of this newfound expertise.

Young as he was, he suspected, believed there to have been a hard-to-explain, coalescence of minds—a blending of minds. He felt she also knew exactly what had happened.

Jéjé Barnard probably never figured out how clever this woman really was. Sister Eugenie might well have heard the voice of God inside her own head. George still doesn't really know what happened during that after-noon.

It was weird, awfully weird. For many years, he tried to lock it out of his mind. What fourteen-year-old boy would want to relate to a nun? Jeez! You'd have to have a really big problem if you did.

George's Dutch grandpa was a dowser. He was good at it, and his services were much in demand. For the price of a cigar and a cup of strong coffee, Grandpa would find you an under-ground stream of "sweet water" and tell you how many arms' lengths below the surface it was. All he needed was a fresh, forked willow branch.

That branch "told" Grandpa what he want-ed to know. It even told him where you could find your lost wedding band. The branch would wig-gle up and down when pointed in the right direc-tion, even if the item of jewelry was high up in a thieving magpie's nest.

Doing things like that made Grandpa a very respectable person in the district.

His second eldest daughter, George's Mama,

had a huge repertoire of psychic abilities, but not all of them were greatly reliable. However, she could tell at a glance if a pregnant woman was carrying a girl, or a boy. Unerringly, also, she predicted the weather, a week or so in advance. And if she heard of a missing child, anywhere at all, she would instantly know if it was alive or dead, drowned in a well, or canal, or safely back with its mother on the following day.

Knowing these things made George's mother a very respectable person.

Despite the fact these gifts somehow bothered George's Papa, he had married her, and always loved her very much. But it would be fair to say that he sometimes "came down hard" on his George Mathieu.

Views of a distant future were pipe dreams. Predictions of who would visit the following day were lucky guesses. To the father, information the boy gathered in astral flight was simply dreams.

Frequently, Theodore Barnard denied the proven accuracy of the boy's "other-time-frame" observations. And if his son ever woke up to the real world, he might actually achieve something one day.

Doing these things did not make George Mathieu a respectable small person.

His Papa would never be told about what that crazy Sister Eugenie had done, not by his son. George had long ago clamed up. Somehow, some way, he would figure it all out for himself. He had to. The need to know was an all-engaging compulsion that drove his mind to explore.

The sister Eugenie enigma was still bouncing around inside his skull, looking for an answer.

15

"You Must Let Go"

As the principal of her school, placed in that position of authority by the order to which she belonged, Sister Eugenie could hardly be seen as a crackpot. She was efficient, and the attained level of education rose dramatically under her guidance, whilst she still managed to teach her own class full time.

How nuts could the woman be?

She was in her middle fifties when she so greatly embarrassed George, in her late thirties when she proclaimed to her class the voice of the Creator could clearly be heard.

If she was listening to the voice of her Spiritual Self, her statement could hardly be said to be totally untrue. Sister Eugenie, George presumed, had achieved that difficult, but attainable balance. That balance where Spirit and mind have gone into a most profitable enterprise together. Time and Eternity were pooling their individual resources to realize a common goal. George would be witness to the reality of the existence of the end product of their combined labors.

He just didn't know it yet.

He had had enough for the day. At three-thirty in the afternoon, he did not want to remain in his factory. He wanted to go home, play with his children and talk to the Spirit Guardians.

"It is the old story, Bzutu," George suggested to the Guardian. "If the mountain will not come to Mohammad, the Prophet himself must go to the mountain. So, here I am. Got you, at last. This planet swarms with mortals in plague proportions, and there are no more places for you to hide, but good Spirit Guardians are hard to find."

A little humor might cheer him up, George thought. What a dumb, optimistic assertion that turned out to be.

It had been a lengthy job to find ABC-22—thirty minutes of diligent searching in a trance. He felt the Guardian might have been busy elsewhere, and he had gone to look for him instead of waiting for him to make his presence felt. Wherever it was, George had now arrived. They could be anywhere at all. George could only just make him out. But the ancient Sentinel was clearly not enthralled, neither by his presence, nor by his jokes.

"It was only yesterday, when we jumped from the trees and scuttled about on all fours," the mortal reminded the Spirit Guardian. "How rich do you expect our humor to be, Bzutu? Give us time to evolve. Meanwhile, give us a little credit for trying to be entertaining," he suggested.

The look on his face told of his feelings as the mighty Warrior turned to face him and seemed to sigh. The spear, that most deadly looking weapon, was switched from his right hand to his left. George so hoped he did not want to poke it in his direction. That awesome, shimmering business end of the spear still worried him each time he faced the Warrior.

"So many wake-up calls," he reminded ABC-22, "What are they about, my friend?"

"We guide you," was the mind-to-mind answer.

"Have you popped the details in my mind already?" George asked.

"It is done," the Guide's answer came.

"I'm only human. I have concerns about what I am in for next, Bzutu," the mortal admitted. "Even our own shadows make us jump, you know. Now . . . that would never happen to you, would it now?"

Even before he had said it, the Guardian was smiling. At last! But it was mostly to make his pet mortal feel good, George figured. As always, the Spirit Warrior was reading his mind. Only George's fickle, spur-of-the-moment flashes had ever surprised ABC-22 in the past.

"You spoil all my jokes by picking my brain," the human complained. "And I still don't know what those wake-up calls are all about. Can't you let the occasional cat out of the bag?"

"You will know very soon," the Guardian's mind told him.

George nodded pensively. He knew it was probably best not to know, and just let it happen. ABC-22 knew he was just another curious human. The Spirit understood the concept of apprehension, but he did not comprehend the feelings that came with it. Fear was to be dealt with, and apprehension about the future was such a waste of time, energy, emotions.

"I will try to have a little more faith," George suggested. "I know you Guys will always look after us."

"Ever!" came the instant mind-to-mind reply. ABC-22's attention was needed elsewhere on the planet. Duty called. He needed to send George away.

"Give everyone my love," George told him quickly. "Their favorite pet vertebrate greets them all. Now quickly tell me the winners of the first three harness races for tonight, old Friend," Barnard suggested jokingly. "Please, Bzutu? I love to win and be home early."

"We guide you!" came the impatient, spoken answer.

"I'll split my winnings with you," the mortal laughed.

"Sleep. We guide you." ABC-22 was gone. Or George was back home. Whichever. It was hard to say where in time and space the two minds had met.

"Okay! Okay!" Don't try bribery, he thought. This Warrior can never be bought. And do as you're flipping well told, when you're told and how you're told.

That very same night, George was looking the Spirit Guardian in the eyes. He could see him as clear as day now. Standing right beside him, he appeared to be quite pleased with George—the Warrior's very own mortal apprentice. This was much better than a few days prior at San Francisco Bay. Excellent perception!

And no doubt, the large group of Entities surrounding someone's deathbed was lending their minds to the entire procedure. George could never achieve this level of observation by himself. That was obvious.

He eyed the group cautiously. Not until that night did he ever see so many Spirits in one crowd. Some were no bigger than a four-year-old child, and some were much bigger than the human. There were two of most of them, but not of all. They were clever! Here was millions of IQ in mind power gathered in one place. Smart as they were, they weren't looking down on a mere mortal. These twelve, perhaps fourteen or more Spirit Onlookers had respect for all creatures.

Some of them seemed to be standing inside the stones of the wall, just to be able to surround Sister Eugenie at the head of her bed. She was dying, and clinging to life, both. And if you didn't know that it was Sister Eugenie, no one would blame you, but George already knew it was she. She knew someone had arrived, though her eyes were closed. She didn't know whom it was that had come to visit her. Suddenly George had doubts, and he reached out momentarily to touch ABC-22's shoulder.

"We are in Bavaria?" the mortal asked.

"We are all here," the Spirit Guide answered. Moments later George glimpsed the rolling green hills, some barren, harvested rye fields, then a view of the convent from the outside. Next up, he was back inside the room. He needed to think. If it's midnight on the other side, late Spring at the bottom of the world, it must be daytime in Bavaria and late Fall at the top of the world. The rye is already harvested.

It all seemed to fit.

"This is not a lucid dream, eh, Bzutu?" he asked, just to make sure. "And this is "now" time? Professor Willis said I must know where, and when in time I am."

"We are all here," the Spirit Guardian repeated. "And this is now."

George walked closer to the bed. He needed to take in the material scene. This time, he felt unrushed. There was a young sister, dressed in all white, to Sister Eugenie's right. One would call her a novice, he thought. There was an old nun close to the patient's left. These two oldies had long been friends, but she would not hold the dying patient's hand and Sister Eugenie needed that. Pumped full of morphine, all her powerful beliefs had become uncertainties. She knew she was dying, but she was now afraid to go on with it.

George wondered what was killing her, apart from old age. Instantly, he could see it all: A worn-out body and a network of intrusive tissue that had invaded her body, more so on her left than on her right. Stacks of it! She was emaciated. Triggered by a shortage of trace elements and a defunct immune system, it looked like cancer, but it was the wrong color. It was white. Cancer was black, pale brown if it was benign, but likely to turn malignant in the future. He had seen both, and many times.

He turned back to the Warrior. "Bzutu, is that cancer of the lymphatic system?" he asked.

"It is so," the Guide answered.

George needed to know more. "My body and brain are in my bed?" he suggested. "The rest of me is here, yes?" he asked. "That will explain things for me."

"It is so," the Spirit Guardian answered him again.

Someone was looking after his body, he felt sure of that now. It was being cared for on life support. It meant his Spirit Self, mind and soul, complete with identity and personality, had made the trip halfway around the globe. Sister Eugenie would recognize him for sure.

"Pretty clever of you to get the lot of me transported out here," George complimented ABC-22. But the Guardian didn't want to confirm all that.

"Go about your task," ABC-22 ordered. George's questioning, it seemed, was holding up the procedure for the entire congregation.

"You have to let go now and die," the Guardian's apprentice told the nun. "You'll be fine. It's easy. Just let go." Strangely, she was unaware of any of his Spirit Friends being present. Perhaps Spirit Entities have no souls, George thought. But the woman didn't trust George either. She had been hanging in there for days with the stubbornness of that powerful mind of hers.

I will think in German and let her read my mind, he thought. Forgive me for neglecting that language, he prayed. But it was easy! It was still there, all of it.

"Remember Jéjé Barnard," his mind told her. "You must remember Jehanne Colette Barnard, the shy girl who had all those brothers." That wasn't helping much. "You taught her for many years, Jehanne Colette. In the Netherlands. Remember? Try to remember."

They were getting nowhere fast. Some fool had drugged the old dear right out of her loving mind. They would be there forever and one more day at the rate it was going.

It seemed crazy for him to be talking someone into giving up on life. Generally, he was convincing people to hang in there. This was one for the books.

"You're holding up all spiritual progress in the whole universe, Sister Eugenie," he told her. "A busload of Guardian Angels is waiting to take you home," he suggested. But she didn't trust him, and still didn't know him.

"How old are you?" he asked.

She wasn't sure if she was eighty-seven or seventy-eight. She got that all muddled up. She would be eighty-seven, George guessed. She had worked in the Netherlands until she became forgetful, then she had returned home to her convent. At least, she knew that much. Alzheimer's disease, cooking with aluminum pans, perhaps, had played havoc with her brain and mind. The morphine was doing the rest.

"You know me," he tried to convince her. "You know me very well. You know me, and you know you can trust me. I'm telling you, there are many Guardian Angels waiting for you. All you must do is let go."

He looked at the group and smiled nervously at them. He had no idea what, and who they all were. They might feel insulted by being called Guardian Angels. But they sure weren't complaining, or even talking to him.

"You know me," he carried on. "You made a total exhibition of yourself, hugging me inside that examination hall." He thought he would probably blush again if he could.

Suddenly, there was a glimmer of recognition in her mind. She knew what she had done on that day, so long ago. She knew, but it was faint. Again and again his mind took her back in time to the crazy thing she had done. Again and again, he told her she was safe. Time after time, he urged her to let go.

Then, she did let go. Hallelujah! At last! In a blink she was dead. And the "essence" that arose from her body was quickly surrounded by those diverse Entities that had waited so patiently. It felt so good to watch that happen. The next moment, just like that, all of them were gone.

"It is done," said the Warrior.

"She is fine now?" George asked, uncertain, and searching the Spirit Guardian's mind through his eyes.

"It is so," the Guide answered. "Go home, George Barnard," he advised.

"You must be kidding! Under my own steam? You can't just leave me here!" He doubted very much if his

Spirit Self could drag his soul around at the speed of thought. He would need lots of help. But ABC-22 was gone. And George woke up the following morning, in his own bed, but with a lot of questions and few answers.

In his mind he heard ABC-22 say, "So, you don't think we are doing a good enough job, eh, George Mathieu? That's okay. We can handle a little criticism from a poorly informed mortal. Now see if you can do better. I'll bring some of my friends around to witness your imminent failure. Oh, well, you did it. Just your luck you happened to know her, I guess." It was hard to ignore the fact that her extraordinary stubbornness had kept her from moving on.

Who was Sister Eugenie? More to the point, what was Sister Eugenie? If this woman actually witnessed a preview of her own demise, way back then in that examination hall, every aspect of her crazy behavior can be explained. And why not? This universe is a treasure trove of ostensible impossibilities.

But that is only a theory.

All George Barnard is sure of is that he now knows a whole lot less than he thought he did. A theory is what he has, and, sadly, nothing more.

Spirit Guardians like ABC-22 can't dish it all up for us on a plate, fax us the details, or stick it all on the Internet. We are evolutionary creatures, and must find out these things for ourselves. Supposedly, that's half the fun.

Chances are that many of the voices the nun claimed to hear belonged to the likes of ABC-22, or Andréa. But how would she know if she never managed to get a good look at the Guardians? If she never managed to reach out and touch them? Fundamentalist teachings, religious dogma, would quickly override those visions. She might very well have crossed herself or thrown a fit if she saw ABC-22 in her convent. This armed Warrior of the Halfway Realm is truly awesome to behold.

As a species, we are distrustful, prejudiced. Others often insult or shun those who talk to the Spirit Guardians of the Halfway Realm, and call them "walk-ins"—mindless human creatures under the control of an evil spirit.

But Spirit Guardians don't have puppets. They have students, and charges they protect. Their code of behavior is ethical, moral, also complex, but well-structured. And they care for all aspects of the complex human creature.

They are "all ways" vouched for.

16

"Shame, Fergo! Shame!"

Few people smiled as readily, and showed as many pearly white teeth, as did the lively Karina Nicholson.

Poker faced and frowning, George Mathieu stared at the tip of the receptionist's nose. "How do you do **that**, Kari?" he asked.

"What? What? What?" She urgently reached for her mirror and cautiously checked her make-up for blemishes. "Do what, George Barnard?" she asked.

"Look so good . . . as you're chalking up the many years," he told her.

"You are a tormentor," she protested, and then she laughed and said, "I'm only twenty-one. That's all. And if I haven't got it now, I never will have."

He nodded his agreement and would only smile.

"With your honest face, you catch me off guard every time," she sighed. "You couldn't have migrated here. You must have been deported from over there."

"Urgently got rid of," he admitted. "Don't tell anyone, I beg of you."

She was showing him more teeth. "Isn't it a scorcher out there? We're in for a week of heat-wave conditions. Do you want Fergo?" she asked. "Just walk into his office without knocking. He

never knocks, not even on bathroom doors."
Karina disliked Colin Ferguson it seemed.

Barnard didn't know what to think of purchasing manager Colin Ferguson. Colin was a short man and kind of bookish, yet restless in the way his eyes darted about. We all have our problems, and my problem is bigger than his, Barnard mused.

George had quoted on much of Associated Suppliers' requirements and for more than two years failed to procure a major contract. What little he had succeeded in selling Ferguson would scarcely pay for George's many trips to that firm's offices.

Two functioning prototype turntables stood on his desk. For anything as mundane as a turntable, they looked to be well designed.

"Just one hundred of the industrial model," Colin Ferguson told him. "Twelve thousand of the little commercial one. But that's probably too big a challenge for your little company. Anyway, take "em with you," he suggested. "I don't need "em back here until after the weekend. Monday, though, not later."

"The project's not too big for us, Colin," Barnard assured the man. "Come and visit us some time. See how we've grown of late."

Ferguson didn't look like he cared much for the welfare of Barnard's business. He wasn't interested in visiting the firm, it seemed.

"I hope you get it this time, George," he said. He sounded genuine, or well practiced. "Contracts will be awarded two weeks from next Friday, for a deadline of six weeks after that on all of it."

Barnard checked the specifications. "Spun aluminum?" he queried. "Not high-impact polystyrene? That could be tricky with the wiring, Col, but only on the small, shallow one."

"I don't care," Ferguson answered. "The things are approved, stamped and certified."

Barnard took the two working models away with him; strangely certain he would gain this first ever big contract from Associated Suppliers, oddly convinced the small unit was a dangerous toy.

An unusual situation had developed at the works, especially for that time of the financial year. But for one large government order, the Barnard company's job board was clean, a blank. It greatly troubled Production Chief, Kevin Weiss. One could never tell by looking at his face, only by looking at his hands. If his hands were firmly planted in his coverall pockets, Weiss was worried, sometimes angry.

"The capital city will keep us spinning for precisely two weeks," Weiss predicted. "Then we've got nothing. Some potboilers, but really nothing much. And zilch in the pipeline, George."

Barnard looked up to see what Kevin's hands were doing. He could have saved himself the effort. They were in his pockets, naturally, where else? "We'll get this contract from Associated Suppliers," George told him. "Don't worry, Kev. We'll be fine."

Weiss let out a laugh that sounded more like a painful yelp. "Colin Ferguson has never given you anything, and nothing's what you're gonna get this time around," came his scathing remark. "You're dreaming, Barnard."

George moved back in his chair, prepared to stare him down. "You've got the order!" he told Weiss bluntly. "You've got only one problem, Kev. They're unsafe. People will get electrocuted with the things. If production is running smoothly out there, put your time into sorting out the little turntable's wiring."

"Your Spirit Friends in the sky told you that?" Weiss wanted to know. "They came down from a cloud and promised to do magic for you? A miracle is what we need."

He had made George angry about his commenting.

"Both Associated Suppliers," Weiss proclaimed, "and their creepy Colin Ferguson, are our biggest wasters of time. I met him, and I didn't like him. I still don't like him. And, if we were to actually get those two jobs, we'd miss the deadline by two weeks. It would take us eight weeks to complete that order, George."

"Six weeks, and you can do it, Kev."

"Eight weeks at least," he answered.

"Six! Now, switch the flaming things off," George told him, "take the small one apart, and see what you can do. Do it here in my workroom and I'll help you with it."

"Do what the boss man says," Weiss grumbled, "for bloody Ferguson."

Both turntables were identical in shape. One was much bigger than the other. Their stability had been compromised somewhat, but their shape was excellent. They bore the label of a well-known industrial designer. The only thing the smaller unit needed was appropriate channeling, somewhere safe for its straight 240 volts input.

By Friday afternoon the turntables had been in Barnard's workroom for more than twenty-four hours. The two men had taken the units apart many times and put them back together again. But Kevin and George were no closer to solving the problem. The small turntable was simply too shallow for the wiring to be secure, whichever way it was routed.

The electrical wires would need fastening every few centimeters with welded aluminum studs or unsightly pop rivets. This was entirely impractical, and it would be far too expensive. But sooner or later, the wires would move, and the turning part would wear through them. People would get the shocks of their lives.

"I'm coming in tomorrow to sort this baby out," George told Kevin. "I'm treating just one of my patients at nine, and then I'm free. There's got to be an answer staring us right in the face. We're just not seeing it right now."

"I'm coming in, too, George. I'll let them both run all night, to see what happens." He moved to switch on the power, touched the small turntable and received an immediate, but mild shock. It was time to switch the things off. Time for George Barnard to see if Colin Ferguson cared about the project.

"You can talk to the cleaners, the security man, or you can talk to me," Karina Nicholson told him on the telephone. "Better talk to me," she added with a laugh, "I'm friendlier and prettier than any of them, George."

"I want Colin Ferguson, Kari, and I want him now," Barnard insisted.

"He leaves early on Fridays and has an unlisted telephone number, sorry," she informed him.

"Jeez, there's got to be someone there. This is really urgent," he assured her.

"Only old Mr. Bellfield in the big room," was the answer. "He's chairing a directors' and shareholders' meeting. That's why I will still be here till seven this evening. I'm doing the drinks after."

"Get him on the line for me, Kari." Barnard was pressing her to act.

"You must be joking!" she yelled. "He'll cut off my ears if I walk in now. You wouldn't like the looks of me without my ears, Mr. Barnard."

"Stop fooling, Karina," he snapped at her. "We're working on a trainload of turntables for your firm, each of them a potential booby trap. They will electrocute people right across this continent. It will cost your firm millions."

"Jeepers!" she hollered in his ear. "Say it all again and I'll write it down, and then I'll give him a note. I'm allowed to do that."

Karina was gone and back in a jiffy. "Do you want to know what old Mr. Bellfield wants you to do, or do you want to know what he said?" she asked.

"Tell me exactly what he said, young lady," Barnard answered.

"Oh, God," she whispered. She was taking a deep breath. "Get ready for this, George. Old Mr. Bellfield said, "Tell that man to redesign the bloody things. I don't give a tinker's cuss what they're made of, or if he makes them round, square, or triangular, or if they look like crap. As long as they are safe. I hate dead bodies all over the shop. Funerals cost money." That's what he said, George. And I'm ever so sorry. But old Mr. Bellfield used to play rugby, and drink a bit, and that's where he learned to talk like that," she explained.

Karina had made him laugh. George knew Richard Bellfield to be quite old. "He played rugby all right, Kari, forty or more years ago, maybe."

"He said something else, George," Karina added.

"What?"

The receptionist hesitated for a moment. "He said, "I've never bloody well heard of that man, or of his firm. Wouldn't know him from a bar of soap." That's what he said."

Barnard was too stunned to answer her.

"George, that means he has never, ever sighted one of your quotes over the five thousand dollar mark. Everything over five thousand is countersigned by him on all official quotes coming in and orders going out."

"I never heard you say that, Karina."

"There's nothing wrong with my lines!" she suggested smartly.

"Listen to me, Kari!" Barnard told her again. "That information never passed your lips. Savvy?"

"Oh, God," she finally sighed. "Might he be on the take? George? Shame, Fergo! Shame!"

"Probably not," Barnard told her, hoping he sounded convincing. "But, just in case. Don't talk about it, ever."

Barnard knew she got it right. Colin Ferguson was toying with his own and with his family's future, as well as risking a potential jail term.

"We can redesign it," Barnard told Kevin Weiss with a smile. "But they now prefer them to be triangular. Good shape for a turntable, Kevin."

"They're all bloody mad," Weiss grunted.

Weiss and Barnard worked on the design of the little turntable until six on that Saturday. They made precious little progress, went out for dinner, and to rethink the project. So far, they had gone about it all wrong, they agreed. The construction had to suit their capacity and expertise, no longer the original design. They were also in a position to make it a sturdier, more stable and simpler unit, saving their client some money. This might almost ensure they'd get the contract.

Within minutes of their returning to the plant they had it all figured out. The top and bottom segments would come from the very same injection mould. They would make a handsome profit and still shave thousands of dollars off the total cost. This was the kind of task the two men enjoyed most about their jobs: The opportunity to occasionally move beyond the border posts of conventional thinking.

Barnard was happy, but in his mind he was repeating what Karina had said, "Shame, Fergo! Shame!" There could be many explanations for Bellfield not sighting George's quotes, but he guessed Karina Nicholson had it right.

They set about fabricating a new prototype when the power suddenly cut out. Just momentarily, it blinked off and came back on again. The same strange thing happened a few more times. It might be an electric motor, giving its warning of an impending burn-out. Barnard looked around the factory, hoping to find the cause, but he couldn't find anything wrong.

The lights were all on, and the air compressor was running smoothly, together with two of their fully automatic machines. With the blistering heat outside, the air conditioner was going full bore, but its big motor seemed fine. The cause of the glitches was a mystery.

"They are your Spirit Guardians," Kevin Weiss suggested, "telling us we've got the design of this prototype correct. It'll happen again in a moment, and that will confirm we've got the order, George." Kevin Weiss was enjoying himself and surely also secretly feeding his apprehension. Too many of Barnard's predictions had come true, and over too many years, for him to ignore the phenomena.

Kevin was a fearful man.

Perhaps, he doesn't like unauthorized Spirit Guardians wandering around amongst his staff, Barnard mused. He would surely wet his pants if he ever caught sight of ABC-22. The near-naked Warrior was a formidable presence.

Weiss felt even more delighted when the lights blinked again, just moments later. "See! That's it," he commented. "We've got the Associated Suppliers' job in the bag, and we'll even complete it in six weeks. I could get used to those Spirit Guardians of yours."

Barnard knew he never would.

By nine-thirty of the following Monday morning, a courier was speeding towards the offices of Associated

Suppliers with three packages and an envelope. Colin Ferguson would soon receive his two turntables and Kevin and George's gleaming new prototype. The pouch contained Ferguson's paperwork, as well as the quotations, new specifications, delivery schedule and an estimate of the savings he would make on the new design— almost nine thousand dollars.

George expected Ferguson to call him back within the hour, but nothing happened.

By lunchtime both his secretary and the production man walked into his workroom. It seemed an urgent meeting was to be held, as had happened before this day. Lucie brought the piping-hot coffee. Kevin stood planted in the doorway, hands in his pockets. There was no escaping these two, and no excuse to walk out.

"We need to talk, George," Lucie suggested.

"Ferguson is giving us the slip," Kevin Weiss suggested.

Barnard had the distinct feeling that defending Colin Ferguson would be a waste of time. He would soon be defending himself. "We really are going to have to do something now," he suggested vaguely.

"Can I ring some clients, and see what's in the pipeline?" Lucie suggested. "There's no record of the work-on-hand situation ever having been so bad, George."

He sized up the young woman who had only just joined the firm. Not yet twenty-one, Lucie had it all: a catwalk appearance, a charming telephone voice, a head for figures and a love for her new, "adopted" company. What she lacked in experience, she more than made up for in enthusiasm. Lucie was one of the firm's great assets, an achiever. She and her partner had almost paid for their new home.

"We won't get those turntables, George," Kevin stated. "We must look elsewhere."

The production man would never change. Weiss had a permanently pessimistic outlook on life. There was no better carer for the production teams. They were his family, and Kevin was their boss, Barnard was not. Kevin looked the part, always wearing a tie, and "Mr. Weiss" to his younger apprentices.

"I want those turntables," George told the two. "We bloody well deserve to get them after the effort we've put in. If we don't get them, I'm declaring war on Associated Suppliers. I don't care how big they are. I don't care how corrupt they are. It will be a bloodbath, I promise you."

There was a big smile on Lucie's face. Her eyes were sparkling. "We're pretty sure we know what's going on in that firm, George. It's obvious," she stated.

Behind her, near the door, Kevin Weiss paled a little. "George!" he shouted in fear. "That firm is massive. They could break us."

"They could," Barnard agreed. "But I doubt very much they will. And if . . . they, too, will bleed for years, and they'll always remember us. You two go and dig up the last two years of Associated Suppliers' quotations. Tally up all the damned jobs I've ever quoted on for them. Don't miss anything. Give me the thing in a comprehensive, typed report. The man at the top of that organization is known for his shooting straight. I will let *him* have it straight for a change, and by next Friday week, not later."

Kevin did not look happy. He would never find a single one of those old quotes with his hands glued into his pockets. But Lucie would not even finish her coffee.

She was on a mission.

By two o'clock that afternoon, no one in the firm was any longer ready for battle. The ten horsepower motor of the big air compressor had blown up in the heat-wave conditions. More than half of Barnard's work force was instantly out of business, and almost all of them opted to go home. There was a scramble for the telephone lines as they searched the dealers for a new engine.

Their new electric motor, stronger, but smaller, would not arrive until six that afternoon. That's when Kevin and George could finally begin to fabricate a new engine mounting.

It surprised Barnard to still find Lucie in reception at nine thirty that evening. Her partner, Dennis, was assisting her. Kevin and George had the compressor operational again, and Lucie was putting the finishing touches to the Associated Suppliers report.

They were a war party after all.

17

The Fury of the Flame

Doctor Ian Jasper was an absolute whiz when it came to understanding people. With just seven crummy pages of outdated psychology in his old med school curriculum, the gynecologist and general practitioner had little more than his intuition, and years of practice, to rely on.

Juanita Brandt, Jasper felt, would "curl up," "fade away," and make herself a prime candidate for a hard-to-shake-off agoraphobia. Jasper's sharp analysis of the case could not be faulted in any way. Juanita was eating the barest minimum for survival, and worse, she was hiding herself in her bedroom ever since their flat had been broken into. Some thoughtless fool had terrorized the young woman out of her loving Latin mind.

Johan Brandt, a recently arrived migrant from the Netherlands, was at a loss about what to do with his petite, Spanish-born wife. The successful, burly, blond-haired construction worker was considering taking his shy, inky-black-haired bride of just a few months back to Europe, Spain if necessary. But Johan lacked the necessary funds. Juanita had thrived during her time in the Netherlands. Now she might just as well be living on the moon because of that burglar. Juanita had snapped.

But there was progress.

Through one of Barnard's ethnic patients,

the Chilean community was rallying behind Juanita and visiting her regularly. One of them had translated her entire one-hour therapy, induction and all, into Spanish. And, although Barnard scarcely knew what he was saying to her in Spanish, the woman was lapping it up.

Every second week, Tuesdays at eight in the morning, had become Juanita's treasured outing to George's clinic.

Barnard hated murdering the Spanish language as much as he disliked the awkward weekday hour, especially on this important day of likely warfare. He needed to be with his crew. But the battle for Juanita's mind also needed to be won. That morning the young woman finally remembered how to smile.

There was no greater victory.

It was just a short walk from the parking apron to his showroom, no more than forty paces between the air-conditioned V8 and his cool workroom. He hurried along as the intense heat hit him like a suffocating, all-enveloping blanket. It was predicted to become the hottest day of a protracted heat wave that was scorching life's juices out of the entire Australian east coast.

Long-legged Lucie was wandering around with her blouse half undone, and her skirt tucked up into her undergarments. "It's half past nine!" she snarled at her employer. "And if you ever worked for a boss, George Barnard, you would have been fired in one day. You're late! You're always missing when you're most needed."

It was obvious the air conditioning had failed. Already, the office was like a cooker with the sun on its full-width windows. The factory would quickly get even hotter.

"No one would employ me any more," he told her. "I had no option but to start my own company, just to be with nice people like you." Lucie would never know how true it was. His stubborn ways and crazy contraptions of inventions had frustrated more than a few of his dreary-minded past employers.

"I'm going to be in a stinking mood all day." She was giving him fair warning.

"Good!" he told her. "We're at war with Associated Suppliers, remember? A bit of a contribution from you in adrenalin output will come in handy."

Kevin Weiss appeared at the office door in a pair of shorts. The tubby production man looked ridiculous with his short, white, hairy legs. Unfortunately, there were no pockets in the garment. What to do with his hands? And where could his necktie be?

"That's two big motors gone for scrap metal inside of a week, George," he remarked. "I have found a new one, a later model. It is smaller and stronger. We're stuck having to make up a custom mounting. Again! No professional help available for four days at the earliest. Even Brian Sutton can't touch anything for a week. There are breakdowns right across town."

That was a blow. "We'll do it, Kev. I'll help you," Barnard promised. The new high-speed motor would have to track with great precision. Mounting motors was not really their kind of job.

"They'll be walking out of here inside the hour," Weiss predicted. "Most of them have stripped down to their waist, already. Of course, my girls are suffering the most. The spray booth is like a microwave oven, the darkrooms twenty degrees over their temperature. And everyone is drinking iced lemon tea by the gallon."

"When will we see that motor?" Barnard asked.

"It should be here now," Weiss answered. "But they'll all be long gone by the time we've got her going. It may be a blessing in disguise, if we don't get that turntable job."

"We'll get that job, but tell the women to go home," Barnard told Kevin Weiss, "unless they're prepared to work topless in this heat. Any of the men, who feel they are feminine enough to also qualify as females, can leave immediately after them."

"You are such a sexist, discriminatory . . . Oh! Men!" Lucie was giving her boss a dirty look. Then, suddenly, her eyes lit up. "What a corker of an inspiration!" she shouted. "None of them would ever be allowed to live it down if they left with our girls. A masterstroke! I love it!"

Even Kevin Weiss had to admit he liked the idea. He could easily spare five women, not all his "boys." "I'll go tell the girls, now," he laughed. "You can tell them about the topless thing yourself," he grunted at George.

Weiss could be such a stick-in-the-mud.

By eleven that morning, Kevin and George had finally dislodged the burnt-out, heavy motor. Working in the dust, oil and grease of the cramped refrigeration housing, stripped down to their boxer shorts, they looked like chimney sweeps. The effort was deserving of their workers' applause. Even more deserving of some iced lemon tea, they settled on the still cold concrete floor of the workroom for a short break. The new electro-motor seemed to have gone AWOL.

From his spot on the floor, Barnard was facing the digital workroom clock as it ticked over to eleven minutes past eleven. Instantly, he realized he had woken from his restless sleep during the four previous nights and at precisely that time.

He closed his eyes, drifted into a trance, and found himself outside the premises of Victory Repetition Ltd, competitors of more than twice their size. Moments later, he was in their tooling-up department. He had been there only once, but recognized the distant clanging of their presses.

There was his precious prototype turntable on one of their benches. There was the official purchase order of Associated Suppliers for the twelve thousand, and there was a thousand dollar bribe changing greedy hands.

Furious, momentarily unable to speak up, Barnard quickly surfaced from the trance. He had once again become an industrial spy. For only the second time in his life, he was given a clear view of an underhanded deal being worked.

"They took from me all jealousy, all hatred, all care for worldly goods," he told the startled Kevin Weiss. "They left me with a bloody seething anger few mammals on this God-forsaken planet can begin to imagine the power of. This is the Fury of the Flame."

"It's not so bad, George. We can . . . " he began.

"Kev, I just saw Colin Ferguson take a thousand dollar bribe. Those bastards at Victory have got our order *and* our bloody prototype turntable."

"Lucie!" Barnard shouted at the top of his voice. "Thank God I did not send our lass home, Kevin. Now the feathers are going to fly."

"Bring your notepad with you, Lucie!"

She seated herself at his desk, ready to do her shorthand trick, and looking down on her two bedraggled seniors with a self-satisfied smile on her sweaty kisser. That condescending look quickly changed as she started to take notation. Her mouth, seemingly, would close no more. Next to George, the dirt was freely flowing from Kevin's face as the sweat of his fear poured onto his dirty chest and shorts.

"That's it, Lucie." Barnard told the young lady. "Your report, a copy of all our Associated Suppliers quotes, two or three pages of today's positions vacant, a dollar out of petty cash, and that letter. I'll sign it as soon as you give me a shout."

The young woman was ecstatic. "Do you fight a dirty war, or what!" She was drumming her fists on his desk with delight. "Dennis will love it! Can I tell him about it tonight?"

"Check with me," Barnard told her. "All hell will break loose, but maybe not until tomorrow. Just throw me that telephone, Lucie. I'm not getting up yet."

"There may be no tomorrow," Kevin Weiss suggested. "George, that's defamation of character, slander and God knows what else it is."

"It's also very true and very sad," Barnard told him.

"Karina?" he spoke into the telephone. "A courier will hit your place in about forty minutes from now. He will bring you a large envelope. That envelope must go to old Mr. Bellfield and no one else. Will you see that he gets it?"

She promised George she would. Her lunchtime was not until one o'clock, she said.

"Is that George Barnard?" sounded a man's deep voice over the telephone. This had to be Bellfield Senior, an odds-on bet.

"Mister Barnard to you, if your name is Mr. Bellfield," George told the man. "Only close friends call me George. But I don't know you, sir. And I don't know if I would choose to ever know you."

There was a moment of silence, and then the voice came back, together with some muffled background noises. "Mr. Barnard," the voice carried on in measured tone. "I am speaking to you from my office. I am speaking to you through a box that is on my desk, Mr. Barnard. Your voice comes out of this box. It can be heard by all that presently share my office. And I give you fair warning, Mr. Barnard. Included amongst these people are shareholders of our organization, relatives, directors of this organization, and others. Mr. Barnard, my corporate lawyer is also here." It seemed to be all he had to say for the moment. He sounded cold.

Weiss was shaking in his shoes. Lucie was perspiring profusely. We would have to be the sorriest looking bunch of critters on the coast, Barnard mused with a nervous smile. Here I am, putting all of our livelihoods at risk. Bellfield could crush us.

"I'm ever so pleased, Mr. Bellfield, you own one of those boxes," he told the man. "Yours is undoubtedly gold plated. Mine is only made of steel, second-hand, and rusty at the edges. But I, also, have people listening to your voice, Mr. Bellfield. Intelligent people, Mr. Bellfield. I can even put you on public address, so my entire work force can hear your voice. And, Mr. Bellfield, the very youngest of my apprentices may want to know from your esteemed corporate lawyer how it is possible for our firm to save you millions in litigation, for you to then give our prototype to Victory Repetition. Have him tell this to my sixteen-year-old apprentice, Mr. Bellfield. I don't really care to know. Or might you admit that anything remotely representative of moral behavior long ago left your firm, your shareholders and investors, your family and yourself. Perhaps it also left the offices of your esteemed corporate lawyers. You certainly lost it, Mr. Bellfield. Whatever it was you had, you lost it, sir."

"I can crush you like a cockroach!" the man shouted. Now he was angry.

"No, Mr. Bellfield. You are a spent force. It is I who can crush you," Barnard fired back.

"You will hear from me!" Bellfield shouted. Now he was really angry.

"Check the paperwork I sent you, Mr. Bellfield. And be honest enough to let your shareholders know what a mess you're in," Barnard suggested.

"You can prove nothing!" Bellfield was clearly losing control.

"But *you* can, Mr. Bellfield. If you still have what it takes. I do not want to talk with you any more, sir. We, here, have work to do. You will find that it should have included twelve thousand turntables of a greatly superior design, and a saving to you of some nine thousand dollars. Not including years of litigation you would avoid. My apprentice sends you his regards." Barnard cut him off.

"Jesus Christ!" Kevin Weiss swore. He ignored Barnard's angry look.

"I was polite enough, Kevin," George told the production man.

"I'll never forget this day," Lucie remarked with a deep breath. "Never!" She had been holding her breath for far too long. "Can I tell Dennis? Tonight? Please? George?"

"Well, now. That's got to be worth a big, tall, iced lemon tea, all around, yeah?"

She was gone in a flash to get them.

Barnard had set out to upset the Chief Executive of that huge family company, Associated Suppliers. Even if he lost the contract, and he now no longer cared about it, at least he had the devious pleasure of getting even with the firm, as well as with Colin Ferguson.

But even as he spoke with Bellfield Senior on the telephone, his attitude changed. Here was a man who was being ripped off on a daily basis. Barnard felt sorry for him. And instantly he started to wonder how the Spirit Guardians would feel about his having been so crude in his choice of words. Might they expel him once again?

He didn't have long to wait for his answer.

18

"The Filthiest Man"

It was Karina Nicholson who phoned in at twenty past one. She had walked quite a distance away from her office, and in the steaming heat, to make the call from a public telephone. Her message was simple. She had long suspected what was going on in the firm. But torn between her loyalty for the old man, and her fear of losing her job if she blew the whistle, she had remained silent. Karina phoned to say, thank you, and please, don't say I rang. It was hard to escape the notion she was distancing herself from the corruption. It seemed important to her that George should know.

Colin Ferguson had been fired on the spot, she told Barnard, and he had taken much money from his wallet, right in front of her reception desk. He had handed it to Bellfield. The receptionist sounded distressed.

Barnard knew there would be no corporate lawyer making his life a misery. Not likely. Not now.

"Don't believe for a moment Ferguson is the only one, Karina," he told the young woman. "But keep your mouth closed, girl, and your hands out of that cookie jar, always."

"Wouldn't dream of it!" she shouted. "How could you think I would!"

"It's no good for you," he quickly interrupted

her; "it causes rapid aging."

She burst out laughing. The stress was gone. "You caught me off guard!"

"Every time," he laughed.

Barnard wondered if Bellfield had the intestinal fortitude to telephone his firm and the stomach for some humble pie. If he waited till the following day, George would ignore the man.

The electric motor finally arrived and Kevin and George were back in that hot little poke, measuring the distance between bolt holes, arguing about the ways and means, and getting dirtier by the minute. They finally agreed on re-drilling the old plate, when Lucie came to get her boss. A rather pleasant sounding Mr. Bellfield wanted to speak with him, she said. There was an inexplicably delightful glow in the bedraggled young secretary's eyes. She stayed right on his heels, and Kevin was not far behind her.

"You are now wired up with my second-hand, rusty iron box, Mr. Bellfield," Barnard told him.

"The positions vacant pages and the dollar?" Bellfield questioned. "Can you fill me in?"

"You will need to find a new job when your shareholders fire you and some money for the pay telephone to apply for that job by the time I'm through with you," Barnard answered without hesitation.

"I thought that to be the case. We have no war with you, Mr. Barnard," he informed George. He was using Barnard's combat terminology. Kevin and Lucie were visibly enjoying themselves. A few more of their employees were crowding into George's small workroom.

"We will take the shutters from our windows, Mr. Bellfield. The sandbags and the machine gun from our front door, and on your word of honor," Barnard promised him.

"I have checked all your paperwork, Mr. Barnard. And all your quotations have arrived here at least a week too late. Your delivery dates are always one or two weeks over our required time limit for the projects. I must say your prices are mostly acceptable."

This old man is not catching on. He should get out of the game pronto, George felt. "Mr. Bellfield, those submissions and projected delivery times are according to the schedules written and signed by your purchasing officer. Would you like them by courier? We don't need them any more."

Now Bellfield caught on. They could all hear him suck in lots of air and blow it out again. Then, nothing could be heard for quite some time.

"May the merciful Lord forgive me for my failing you all," he said. Bellfield Senior appeared to be having a quiet nervous breakdown. The three confederates could spare him the time. They waited silently. Finally, he came back on the line.

"Will you come over to see me, Mr. Barnard?" Bellfield asked.

"Give me an hour," George casually suggested.

"You are less than thirty minutes away," Bellfield answered, still the dictator.

"I look like something the cat dragged in. I need a shower," George suggested.

"Come as you are," the man insisted.

Two of his bedraggled staff looked like they would start laughing at the wrong time. George warned them off with a critical look. "Did you say come as you are?" he questioned.

"Yes," came the old man's reply. "As you are."

"As I am, Mr. Bellfield. In thirty minutes. As I am right now." He rang off.

"You can't go wearing that!" Lucie cried. "Your shorts! Your dirty underwear!" She tried to stop him at the workroom door.

"You're coming along to make notes," George threatened her.

She stepped back instantly, straightened her skirt, did up a button on her blouse, and smoothed out her hair. That was fun to watch. Then she shouted, "No!"

"George . . ." It was all Kevin Weiss could think of saying.

There was a fleeting glimpse of the near-naked Spirit Warrior as George Mathieu Barnard bare-footed his way over the hot concrete to his car. We'll both go as we are, he thought. He didn't dare say it.

"All deliveries go to the docks around the back," Karina Nicholson informed him. She had mistaken Barnard for another lost trucker who could not find the loading docks if he fell off them, but only for a moment. She stood, sat down again, stood again and stayed standing. "Mr. Barnard," she said softly, absent-mindedly.

"I already knew that was my name," he told her. "I'm seeing a man who knows about bars of soap. He told me to come as I am. And today, this is precisely how I am. I know where he hides himself, Karina. Stay there. I'll see you on the way out."

She was saying, "Oh, my God. Oh, my God. Oh, my God." Then came, "I'm not here. I'm not here. I'm not here." Karina was saying all that whilst seemingly needing to hold her teeth in place. She was still standing there, talking to herself, when Barnard stepped through the carved oaken door and into Richard Jason Bellfield's domain. His was the classiest office the businessman had ever seen.

The silvery-white-haired patriarch looked imposing, even seated behind his desk. The immaculately dressed, middle-aged woman with him had a shorthand notepad on her lap. Bellfield looked long and hard at the intruder. Barnard smugly stared right back at him.

"Who the hell are you?" Bellfield shouted at last.

"Come-as-you-are Mr. Barnard!" George shouted back at him. "At your service! Thirty minutes on the dot! Sir!"

"You are the filthiest man I've ever laid eyes on," he told George. He had just made his first big mistake. Barnard was too well prepared. "And you are the most incompetent creature I ever wasted my time on," came the reply.

That shut the old guy's mouth for a moment. Then he smiled at George, slyly, turned to the woman, and said, "A large jug of coffee, please, Gladys. Hold my calls. We have business."

"And a towel, please, Gladys," Barnard added. "I shall put it on that chair over there, because that's where I will sit." He had taken the initiative. Gladys grabbed up her notebook and seemed instantly swallowed up by the adjacent office.

Suddenly Barnard no longer cared about Bellfield's turntables. Kevin Weiss and all his "boys" could go hungry, for all he cared. He would tell Bellfield what he thought of his organization. The man needed to know what Barnard somehow already knew; it was corrupt from the top management down to the factory floor. He would leave the old fool with a fighting chance to sort it all out.

"I like your style," he suddenly told George. Richard Bellfield had regained his composure. He moved to a large, antique, carved oaken wardrobe, took out an embroidered silken shirt, and held it out to George. "Will you put this on, please, Mr. Barnard. It's not just Gladys," he suggested. "Your state of undress is even unsettling to me." He sounded too genuine, too smooth.

"Pleased to oblige," Barnard responded. He put on the shirt as if his own wardrobe held countless of the two-hundred-dollar shirts. This was a wily old character, this Richard Bellfield. He would turn on Barnard in the twinkling of an eye. This old codger knew the ropes.

"What I would give to have a man like you on my staff," he suggested. "Of course, I'd expect you to wear shoes, and, well, a few more clothes, I suppose."

"I'd be the only one here, looking just the way I do right now, if your air conditioning happened to break down. Your useless lot would be heading for the beach. My crew is still producing while they roast, Mr. Bellfield. You know it. Colin Ferguson is not the only one ripping you off. This is no longer an organization. This is a long neglected flaming free-for-all."

"You can't prove it!" Bellfield was hurting, and turning on the younger man, but Barnard had asked for it.

"I've done enough," Barnard countered, "The rest is your concern. Sort it out at sixty. By the time you're seventy, you won't have the guts."

Bellfield smiled his sly smile. "I'm seventy-two years old. Can I call you George?"

"You can do that, Richard," Barnard rudely answered. They were getting nowhere. This was a shaky truce at best, and it could stay that way. He wanted out of Bellfield's office, back to his factory, and to ever forget about Associated Suppliers.

"Sort it out at seventy," Barnard suggested. "By the time you're eighty, it may be too late."

"By the time I'm eighty, I could still crush . . ." He swallowed his words. Gladys was back with the coffee and a large towel. She put it on the chair George had indicated. The coffee tray and a small, folded note went onto her boss' desk. Nothing was said until she had once more left the office.

"Do you know how powerful we are, George?" Bellfield asked with a smirk on his face.

"Do you know how resourceful we are, Richard?" was the response.

Bellfield busied himself with the coffees. "You sure have got it," he remarked.

"I beg your pardon?"

"You've got it. George, I'm giving you the order for those whirly things. It's only fair, after the bloody fight you put up. You fight a mean old war, son." He gave Barnard a big grin, but George still didn't trust him one bit.

"Six weeks to fabricate the twelve thousand?" Bellfield asked. He looked so genuine.

"It would take us eight weeks," Barnard suggested. "If I still felt like doing business with you, Richard. I would probably end up hating myself if I did."

"Let's make it seven weeks," Bellfield suggested. "We don't want to call Gladys back in for such a minor change." He pushed her typewritten order across his desk. "I actually just finished dictating the details when you graced us with your, let's call it, eminent presence, George," he explained. The old rogue had already made up his mind, hours before. He had also fired another shot, and he loved it.

They drank their coffees and George Mathieu learned of Richard Bellfield's life-long battle with a corruption problem that involved even his own flesh and blood—family he did not have the courage to expel from the firm.

Then Bellfield turned somber. In the end, surprisingly, he shed some tears.

As George was about to leave, the old bandit had one more trick up his sleeve. "I would have let you have eight weeks, if you'd insisted, George," he said. "I have a pen. I can write an eight, even initial it. Considering the fact you saved me a packet of money, and considering I can now root out this corruption problem once and for all, I should give you ten weeks. But I won't. You've got yourself a juicy contract. We're both winning. Six weeks you've got, George Barnard."

"Seven!" George told him. "You cheating old rogue."

The Bellfields' company had been in the family for four generations. Within a few years, it was taken over by a multinational, split up, sold off—no more. The Spirit Guardians had done their part, Barnard had done his bit, Bellfield had failed. The family disintegrated, but perhaps it had been a casualty for years. Only their turntables are still going around like they were brand new.

Barnard serviced the account regularly until the firm was sold. He went to Richard Bellfield's funeral, still wondering why the man sacked all his corrupt staff, to then re-employ the lot of them, "Fergo" included. Old Mr. Bellfield was one man George Mathieu could never understand. He really was a softie at heart. Bellfield would truly let you have the shirt off his back. Barnard knows he would.

He walked out with that shirt.

Pure anger for being cheated out of a well-deserved contract turned to a concern for the old man losing his grip on Associated Suppliers. It happened very fast. But Barnard's behavior towards Richard Jason Bellfield was nevertheless unpleasant. It was blunt. And yet, there was no effort on the part of the Spirit Guardians to stop him. They, and no one else, were responsible for George's knowing how widespread the corruption problem was.

One could almost safely presume they were in agreement with George's actions. Barnard's concerns about being once more expelled from his platoon for misbehavior proved to be unfounded. And perhaps the rookie had never been expelled, just put into disrepair.

Maybe, as Professor Willis had claimed,

there really was an as yet only-part-evolved Power Without Name in this evolutionary universe. A Force that is occasionally half-awakened by consummate anger, extreme anxiety, or a forceful prayer, and capable of giving precisely what is asked for, rather than what was really wanted or needed.

19

Andréa

Ask yourself what you would do if you met a truly androgynous individual in the streets. Not the somewhat less masculine male who prefers to cook up "lovely meals" and knit his own socks, not him. Not the somewhat less feminine female who wears a business suit, and closes every deal with a hard sell, not her.

We're talking about the physical body kind of androgyny—a person both male and female—with much facial hair and large breasts.

Would you tip your hat to say hello? Would you feel strangely inhibited and quickly cross the road? Would you feel sorry for that individual or perhaps suggest the jeers and insults of a sideshow for an instant improvement of his/her/its self-esteem? Or would you simply ignore him, or her, or it—whatever?

And if he, she, or it then walked into your clinic, would you write Mr., Mrs., Ms., Master, or Miss on the new patient's file, your data-sheet and appointment book? See? You don't really know, do you?

You're not alone.

Meeting up with the Spirit Guide, Andréa, in Barnard's occasional personal playground, the Temporal Halfway Realm, caused him many of those "I'm in two minds about you, friend" moments.

At one stage and in sheer ignorance of her task as a celestial-mortal communicator—a real live telephone exchange and vision of the past and future transmitter—the mortal asked her to get with it, or shove off pronto. That was very wrong of him.

Truly, if a Creator, in all wisdom, needs a creature just like that, then who was George Mathieu Barnard to argue with the Boss?

But that's essentially what he did.

Ted Willis was sipping his mineral water and Louise was already making coffee when the still sleep drunk Barnard finally stumbled into his living room. His visitors were dressed and ready to go thirty minutes before time.

"Tumut is too far away," George suggested, yawning. "Too far to go, just to eat a dead mountain trout. They make those endless highways out of bitumen, you know. And bitumen stretches in hot weather. And between here and there gets to be a kilometer further every day."

"Into the shower with you!" Louise ordered. "That'll wake you up. I'll have your drink ready when you come out and the car's all packed, ready to go." She turned to Ted Willis. "George hasn't changed one bit. He still fools around like an adolescent."

"Car's all packed, is it, Lou Lou? Well, suppose we better go then," Barnard told them.

"Scoot, George Barnard," she yelled after him, "and be quick!"

"Have it hot, then turn it on cold," Barnard grunted to himself as he almost stumbled into the shower. The shower rosette started to fire its scolding hot water at him and he was beginning to feel more awake.

"Louise, girl, you're a marvel," he rhymed. "Your trip to Tumut's sold. I'll have it hot and have a soak, then turn it icy cold." He was coming alive now, but not feeling much better about the long drive ahead. He reached for the soap and lathered up.

"Hi-ho, hi-ho-wo-wo," he sang, "to Tumut we must go. We keep on driving all night long, five hours in a row."

Perhaps as much as six hours, he thought. Perhaps longer? Now, wait on! Why should it take longer? It has never taken me anywhere near that long.

"We couldn't let our Catherine down, we're gonna do this drive. The car's all packed, Louise says, come sun-up we'll arrive."

"No, we won't!" Barnard had said it, loudly, and it had sounded so definite. What a ridiculous thing to say, he thought. But then, abruptly, there was a brief vision of the convention center's driveway and its busy parking grounds. The distinctive metallic-gold Barnard's V8 was nowhere to be seen.

"You're not even going to get there," said an unheard voice, although it sounded ever so clear in George's mind.

"Good grief!" He suddenly felt very much awake, deeply concerned, and so very responsible for his passengers. Perhaps the car will break down on the way, yes, he wondered? No, that's not it. This was serious business and again, a glimpse of the parking grounds failed to reveal the V8. He turned the water mixer fully to the left. "Woorree! This stuff is cold!"

"I don't feel good about this trip, you guys," Barnard told his companions.

Louise handed him his coffee. She, also, looked uncertain to him. He sipped the piping hot life-giving brew slowly, saying, "I've done that stretch of road often enough, but this time, I can't see us arriving at the other end." He sipped some more of the coffee and mulled over what he had seen and heard and felt.

"We could leave ten minutes later than we planned," Louise suggested. She instantly changed her mind, "No, that won't work either." She picked up her cup and joined Barnard on the settee. "It's a funny thing, George," she confessed, "but I haven't felt good about this trip for days. Maybe if we wait half an hour?"

"A delay isn't going to fix it, Louise. This is serious business, this one. Not just a vehicle break-down." He cast a questioning look at the professor.

"You had better zap out and take a peek at it, George," Ted chimed in at last. "I'm sure you are meant to get to the bottom of this."

"Okay. Right now." Barnard dropped a pillow on the armrest of the settee. "Give us this space here, Louise, but stay with us, please. I'll shortly know what's going on. Oh, and don't chuck the rest of my coffee out. I'll still drink it."

She took their cups and watched him stretch out on the settee. To George Mathieu it felt like old times with the three of them there. It felt good to once again be together as a team, regardless of their doubts about the trip. They would soon know what was going to happen. There was an inescapable sense of urgency about the need to talk to the Spirit Guardians.

Barnard drifted towards the time-realm of the Guardians, saying, "I greet you all, you Guys." The mighty Sentinel showed no movement, no emotion. The

Androgynous One turned with great difficulty to look the mortal in the eyes. George realized Andréa was once again bridging the gap of massive time-frame dissimilarity. Even with his now being deeply entranced, he knew Andréa was doing almost all the work of establishing contact, and she was laboring with the effort. It was only the second time Barnard discerned those all-knowing eyes.

There was something he had to quickly say to her, "Will you forgive me for telling you to shove off," he asked of her mind. "It's long ago, Andréa, but I'm still truly sorry I said that to you. People have so many fears and I'm not different when I see you're half of each sex."

"You are all ways forgiven," was her answer. Then she surprised the mortal by saying, "I am a virgin of the Gods."

What a great way to explain the absence of reproductive prerogatives and androgyny, Barnard thought. But there was little time to think. A torrent of information now flowed into his mind.

"Never you mind, my friend," he finally acknowledged all that had come from her great mind. "I understand. You can be such a depressive at times. You worry far too much, Andréa. But thank you all the same."

"Phew!" he suddenly made as she began to show him her pictures of the future. Wow! A head-on smash! A still shot of his station sedan loomed ominously. It was partly crushed, a long way down from the road and precariously wedged against a tree. Then, a deep-red mark appeared in the middle of the picture and it grew bigger, until all of it was red.

He passed on the information to his companions as it came into view. "It's a whopper of a head-on smash," he remarked coldly. "All of the front with part of the driver's side of my vehicle is smashed in. We've come down from a high shoulder in a patch of hilly country. We're stuck against a tree, pointed in the wrong direction. We're pointing northeast! Pointing the way from where we came."

He finally opened his eyes and blinked. Only then did he begin to fully grasp the shocking reality of what he had witnessed. "Cripes! I'm high up above the road-deck and I can't get near the car. Gosh! I'm too bothered to come close, because some of us are dead in there. Me included."

"Where's the accident, George?" Ted asked. It looked like he was remaining calm, yet Barnard sensed his concern, as well as his determination to depart for Tumut, to beat the odds, and to attend the convention. Louise looked very frightened, but she, too, wanted to know more.

"I'll check it on the map," Barnard suggested. He drifted back in seconds. "Give us the map, please, Bzutu, for you are the closest, most powerful and cooperative of all who belong with us." The rookie turned to the reliable, majestic Warrior as a matter of course. "It's much easier for you than it is for Andréa," he suggested, despite his being uncertain which of the Guardians produced the maps.

The distant Androgynous One had many gifts, which were hard for her student to take in. She did have much love and care, and she was a brilliant communicator, but she lacked business sense and had no grasp of urgency, Barnard felt.

The map lit up almost instantly on the screen of his mind and the car traced a thin white line as it progressed at top speed towards its destination.

"Here's Picton," George told Ted and Louise, "Mittagong . . . Bowral . . . Moss Vale . . . here's Goulburn. The car looks fine. What's this? Oh, that was Collector. Blink and you miss it. We're on the Federal Highway now. Water... Lake George! That's it. We're fine until just past the lake."

Again, the still-shot of the company's V8 at its precarious angle flashed before the screen of his mind. It was followed by a segment of high-speed action. A white sedan came tearing over the hill and around the bend. Then it almost completely disintegrated without hitting anything at all.

"Here's the culprit, Ted," said Barnard. "Let us just wind him back and slow him down. Here he is. On the wrong side of the road. There is a young man in this car. Looks like an old Valiant. Yes it is. An old white Valiant sedan, maybe it's cream or yellowish. It's dark here all of a sudden."

Again, the vision returned and the Valiant disintegrated. A red spot now appeared in the center of the wreckage of the car. It slowly spread outward from the center.

"Is that blood?" Barnard asked.

"No, not blood," said an unheard voice. He surfaced from the trance.

"He's dead for sure, this young fellow. His car is in pieces," Barnard informed the two. "I know exactly where it is, too. I know that very spot in the road. He's got to be doing over a hundred kilometers per hour. Too fast, and he's on our side of the road. He's flying!"

Louise seemed less certain about going on the trip. "Do you still want to go after seeing all that, George?" she asked.

"Sure, Louise, or Catherine will be thirty-nine for the rest of her life," Barnard joked.

"What do you intend to do about the smash?" Ted Willis asked.

"We'll go from here to Goulburn," Barnard answered, "then we'll drive the rest of the way from Canberra to Tumut and skip that tricky bit between Goulburn and Canberra. Easy! No smash-up. And it will save us a lot of time as well." He gave the professor a big grin.

Louise had completely lost her composure. "It's hardly a laughing matter, George!" she shouted at Barnard. "Can't you be serious, just for once? Our lives are at stake!" She was exasperated about his apparent insensitivity, unaware of the dilemma George was facing and the uneasiness he was trying to hide.

"George, I would rather not know these things of the future and begin to lead an ordinary life for a change," she pleaded with him.

"I *would* rather know," he grunted at her. "And we haven't left yet, have we?" His voice had sounded rather abrupt. "I'm sorry, Lou Lou," he said. "Just let me clear my mind, for there was something else I saw." He was wondering what was going through Ted's mind. The old genius was remaining awfully quiet.

⌒⌒)

Once again he drifted back to the Spirit Guardians. Urgently, he inquired; "What's that red splotch, you Guys?" He was addressing them all, and the red mark reappeared almost immediately.

Slowly, ever so slowly, the red mark grew and then distorted itself into the shape of a little bright red motor car, travelling sedately south-southwest on the Federal Highway. Barnard kept pace with it and looked inside it. Only one fellow was inside. He was old and frail, clutching the steering wheel and peering into the darkness.

"You did pick a dark night for your travels, old-timer," George tried to tell him. "You are drowsy and as blind as a bat. You're going to nod off to sleep and crash as well, you silly old codger." The man drove on, slowly, unable to see much of the roadway ahead. "I'm not seeing you right now, am I, old fellow?" Barnard concluded. I'm only being shown what's going to be. That's got to be it."

"Your responsibility!" Unmistakably, this was the somber voice of ABC-22. "The safety of you and yours are also dependent on the saving of their lives."

"We're on our way, Bzutu." Barnard surfaced in a hurry and was ready to leave. "Let's go, Ted. Come on, let's go, Louise." He grabbed the half-warm coffee and gulped it down. "Come on then, Louise. We're on our way."

She stayed planted in her chair. "What about the smash! Cripes! George!"

"There will be no smash. We've been given something that must be done. Come on, let's go. We'll be fine, Louise."

She was not going to move. "I don't know!" she cried out.

There would soon be tears from the mother of two, Barnard thought. "Trust the mighty warrior with the code and number printed on his flak-jacket," Barnard told her with an encouraging smile. "He doesn't fool around. I do all of that for him."

"I don't know *any* warriors, George."

"Yeah, but I sure do."

Almost all of us, if not all of us, have intuitive flashes at least at some time in our lives. Can this be our mind, transcending time? Can this be the work of our Spiritual Selves—these Gifts from the Gods whose home remains Eternity but who are simply on work-experience assignment with mortals, for a time, and in time?

Barnard doesn't really know precisely how it works.

What he thinks is that Karl Jung's "Collective Unconscious," the seat of Universal Consciousness and the "Intellect" dwelling in the Halfway Realm may be one and the same thing. But the domain is not sterile, disinfected, or devoid of life. The Halfway Realm literally teems with a more "electrical," less material life. And those who dwell there, like ABC-22, Andréa, Emenohwait the Healer, and the Seraph, Juliette, are the mortal's closest Friends, brilliantly minded and imminently trustworthy friends.

At times a rather scarce commodity on this planet.

20

The Car at the Lake

During the many years of counseling people, generally the most caring and sensitive—often also the most troubled individuals of our intricately mixed races—George Barnard found many with a latent psychic ability. On a few occasions when great talent was evident, he taught them to enter another dimension in time, the domain of the 11:11 Spirit Guardians.

So often, their very first efforts ended in their finding little more than mere figments of their imagination. But there is a certain limit to everyone's imagination. Sheer perseverance will, in the end, bring visions of the future and the past, anytime, and anywhere at all. And these visions tend to become stronger and more accurate with time and practice.

His students learned to become the masters of their time. The therapist was simply carrying on with the work of Professor Dr. Edward Willis.

Ted had made himself comfortable on the back seat of the car. He had insisted Louise take the more comfortable front seat. He had closed his eyes, but he often did that, just to think more clearly. Ted Willis would not fall asleep.

Louise was the restless one. She seemed to have little faith in George Barnard and the Spirit Guardians, and perhaps Louise had long ago said farewell for the last time to her very own Spirit Guide called John.

Already, they had turned onto the highway and the engine responded with a contented purr to the demand for more speed. They were now climbing old Razorback Mountain.

Louise could wait no longer. "George, what is it we have to do?" she asked.

Barnard negotiated a few more tricky bends before answering her. "There's an old fellow in a little red car on the Federal Highway, and he's going towards Canberra. His car looks like that little red delivery vehicle my firm used to have, remember?"

"Vaguely I do," she answered.

"Well, it looks like that, only smaller still. We've got to keep the old guy awake, or he'll crash. If we manage that, we'll be fine, too."

"That's insane, George! That's like blackmail." There was both anger and disbelief in her voice.

On the back seat, Willis was clearing his throat to speak. Then he must have thought better of it.

"It's my job," Barnard told her. "The Spirit Guardians, and only occasionally with my help, change the projected or known course of an event. We cooperate and that's how it goes, Louise. Minds greater than ours may well have concluded that this is the only trade-off we can go for. Positive outcomes all around instead of chaos."

"A depression lifted, for a Miss Jamieson freed? A trade-off. Balance," Ted Willis remarked. "George knows what I'm saying, Louise. He's got it right."

She was silent for a while, brooding. "You mean to say we are buying our lives by keeping him awake? The lives of the three of us in return for the one life of that old man?"

"No! Well, yes. Kind of. Plus the life of that young idiot who is low-flying near the lake," Barnard answered. "Don't forget him. More to the point, a total of five lives saved for some energy expended, if I can figure out what to do."

"That's utterly flaming ridiculous!" she almost spat at him after some thought. "I have heard some crazy things in my clinic, but this beats the lot. Yes! I think I've heard it all now, and then it had to come from you, George Barnard."

"He's got it right, Louise," Ted repeated. "The balance must be maintained and we don't necessarily know what keeps that balance. Have faith."

Barnard tried to work out what Ted could have meant by balance, then decided to stay with the driving. "Suit yourself, Louise," he answered her. "I don't know everything. I do as I'm told, as befits a rookie member of a Spirit team. It may seem like blackmail to you, but it isn't. Not really. It's different, complex, and most unusual this time, I grant you that. It's a temporary hand-over of my free will prerogatives. That's all. It doesn't hurt."

They were passing through the charming township of Picton. None of them had spoken a word for some time. There was no feeling of urgency about the matter in George's mind. Not yet. But there was also no doubt. The visions and warnings had come through so strong and clear, so powerfully obvious, only a courageous fool would disregard this view of the future. I am no longer a courageous fool, Barnard thought. Quite bright, but timid, especially after the Jennifer Sutton disaster.

"How are you going to keep this man awake, George?" Louise suddenly asked.

"I don't know yet. I've got to think of something soon. I'd better."

"Thirty kilometers to Mittagong, George," Louise informed Barnard. "It said so on that sign back there. Do you remember we each got a pie at the university's restaurant years ago? And there was something in it or something wrong with it? Remember? It made us itchy all over and we scratched ourselves raw. You could do that to him."

"What? Sell him one of those moldy old pies?" George laughed. "They've just sold the last of that killer batch an hour ago, Lou Lou. Too late."

"No. I mean you could make him itch all over. Make him scratch. That should keep him awake. It kept me awake all that night."

"What a good idea! What a whopper of an idea! Yeah, that will do the trick. I'll never forget that night, but I don't care if it sends him half mad, as long as he sticks with the driving. What do you think of that one, Teddy Willis?" George asked.

"Brilliant thinking, Louise," Ted praised her.

"Help me with it, Louise," Barnard suggested. "Make him itch like crazy."

"I don't know how to do that! That's your shaman's department."

"Put your mind to it, Louise, it will help me."

"I'll try," she grunted. "Man, you're different."

"Louise, with the enthusiasm, the energy and zest of my youth, I undertook to learn and understand all there is to know in our far-flung universes. There was never a doubt in my puny little mind I could achieve this. Someone took pity on me, and threw me a rope from way up above. And I climbed the rope, all the way into the sky, and I met up with the Great Biami."

Willis chuckled about Barnard's referring to the initiation of the Kadaicha Man of the black Australian tribes. The professor would have "met up with the Great Biami" many long years ago. But Louise did not understand the metaphor.

"I thought I knew you, George Mathieu," she said. "Now I think you've lost the plot in all those years I haven't seen you."

Barnard was undeterred by her remarks. He went on, "The Great Biami showed me all there is to know so I could sense that total comprehension would be far beyond the power of mortal man's mind. The joke's on me, Louise. Where some may see the flash of a glow-worm in a small meadow, I saw a brilliantly blazing torch, but in an infinite number of dark universes of the unknown. The joke's on me. Right now, all I can hope for is that some day, when my Spirit and soul are one and the same I can begin to grasp what it's all about. Meanwhile, I trust that on occasions—just every once in a while—I can provide the Gods with a bout of laughter at my expense. I shall not begrudge them their fun."

Ted laughed heartily, and then quickly clarified his unruly cackling was not indicative of his having become a God. He was too young by far for such a promotion.

Louise felt differently. "If you hadn't always been one of my most caring friends, George Barnard, I would tell you right now that you are by far the strangest man I've ever met. I don't savvy you at all."

Aware of the fact the old-timer was now itching all over and occasionally scratching himself as his little red car ambled along, they drove on without talking. They made a pit stop in Goulburn and poured themselves a drink. Soon after, the V8 gobbled up the many kilometers to the Federal Highway junction.

"I feel itchy just thinking about how itchy he must feel," Louise complained.

"Then you're doing it right," Barnard told her. "Stay with me and keep it up. I'm watching this poor old guy and our whammy sure is working. He can't nod off like that."

They traveled on in silence for a while until Louise spoke again. "I can see the lake. That's it over there, and now we had better slow down, please?"

"Forget it, Louise," George told her. "The one and only hazard is near the southern end of the lake, as we get into hill country again. Keep working on the old timer and I will too." But he eased off a little on the accelerator, just to please her. She was obviously spooked by a potentially predetermined fate that was now fast approaching.

They lost sight of the lake and were moving into hill country. The V8 was now only crawling along the deserted highway, half on the gravel shoulder, half on the asphalt. Ted was keeping an eye to the rear, just in case someone else might be travelling in the same direction at this unlikely hour. The big car had almost slowed to a stop.

Barnard switched the lights on low beam and turned off the heater fan. But for the gentle purr of the engine, one could almost touch the silence of the very early hours of the late summer's morning. They were only a short distance away from the very spot of his visions. With the windows wound down, he strained to hear what his mind told him must soon become audible.

"I think I can hear something, George," Louise remarked. She, too, was listening intently.

"Yes," he told her. "Sounds a bit like someone screaming. Tires! Here he comes!" Barnard yelled. He shocked the V8 into action and it almost leaped off the road deck onto the very edge of the gravel safety strip. Rapidly blinking flashes from a pair of headlights knifed their way through the stands of trees. A white flash darted over the hill and ripped around the bend on the very edge of their side of the road. A shock wave of air hit their car, and they all instinctively raised their arms for protection.

"Holy Mother of God, save us," Louise prayed as the white flash roared past. Then she looked back at the speeding car as it tore around the next bend. "I think that was . . . a Valiant, George . . . yes, it was for sure!"

"It was. I saw the grille. How fast did you think he was going?" George asked her.

She put both hands on her chest, trying to breathe deeply. "What an idiot! I reckon about . . . a hundred and fifty . . . kilometers. My . . ."

Barnard turned in his seat and spoke to Ted, "How close do you think he got, Ted?" he asked. But Ted was watching Louise's behavior with great interest. He didn't answer.

Louise answered for him. "I wouldn't like to say. From here, George . . . my, my . . . what an idiot! We would all have been dead . . . if we'd been on the road."

"Nothing surer, girl," George told her. "It would have been a head-on smash." Again he turned to speak to Ted. "What color did you think it was? Was it white or cream or a pale yellow?" He eased the V8 back onto the road and brought it up to speed.

"Who cares!" Louise suddenly shouted. "Who gives a damn what bloody color it was!" She was looking pale and distressed.

Barnard glanced in the rear-vision mirror and saw Ted smiling. The professor wouldn't answer. Louise's behavior was intriguing him so much.

"Don't go so fast!" Louise was shouting at George. "I'm rattled!"

"Relax," he told her. "That deal back there, that was it, Louise. There's nothing else coming our way between here and the capital city. Trust me. We'll be fine."

"Spooked I am. I've had it! Gosh, I nearly died of fright, Georgie," she cried out. Tears were now rolling down her cheeks.

"Did you wet your pants then, Lou Lou?" he asked her and laughed.

"Don't be stupid!" she shouted, suddenly turning on him. "You can say such stupid things! Dumb you are!"

"Yeah, I know I'm stupid, but I'm alive. We all are. A good fright now and then keeps you healthy, Louise. This close call will keep you looking young and beautiful for many years," Barnard assured her.

"What an idiot you are!" she shouted.

It was good to see Ted Willis secretly enjoying himself so much with her antics. He would always remain a keen student of human nature, and Louise was far from hiding her innermost feelings. Not at any time did Professor Willis show any sign of panic or fear. That was hardly the case with George Mathieu; although the therapist's casual behavior might have been mistaken for his being a cold-blooded, risk-taking daredevil. Barnard began to slowly realize, and was simply overawed by, the accuracy of the advance information and visions supplied by Andréa and ABC-22. He fell silent.

Hold-ups considered, they were making good time. Just ahead, a small red vehicle turned off at Northbourne Avenue and rolled into Phillip Avenue, Canberra.

"Look at that," Louise shouted. "There he goes! That must be him! Not yesterday, not tomorrow, but in real now time. I'll be..."

No one commented on the obvious.

According to the deeply entranced Louise Hewitt, the near-sighted old-timer in the little red car was precious "merchandise" to his fatherless grandchildren, one of whom would become a great achiever. But they all really needed him. The young Valiant driver, only an hour before, had broken up with his steady girlfriend. She had called it quits. Emotionally devastated, he had atypically become careless about his welfare and the safety of others. His people owned a farm not far from the lake and it was somehow essential for this property to be retained by the family. Although rather young, he was generally very responsible, and also their sole breadwinner.

Louise did not have to prove anything to George she had not already proved dozens of times in the years they studied together. Louise was a veritable wizard at picking these things out of nowhere. Feminine intuition, supercharged, high-octane driven, Barnard called it then.

George Mathieu could rarely do what came so easily to Louise Hewitt, and the therapist did not always trust the accuracy of his intuition either.

"Check it out, Ted," Barnard suggested. "Have a look at what Louise just snatched out of fresh air, and tell us what else you get."

Willis' unexpected answer alarmed his ex-students. "I taught you two to use your minds. You each took a different path. I have many gifts for which I'm most grateful, but I can't do any of the things you two were doing," he said. It sounded almost believable.

Barnard veered off the road, too quickly, and stopped the car in a skid. They both turned and looked their old lecturer in the eye.

"You're pulling my leg, Professor Willis," George told him. "You should never say such ridiculous things when I'm driving a car at speed on a pitch-black night. That's tricky!"

"Say you're only joking, Ted," Louise demanded. "Please, Ted?" she pleaded with him. For a moment, it seemed her world was in danger of falling apart.

Briefly, the white-haired old man reached out to her and patted her on the hand. "I listened to all you just said, Louise, and my own Spirit Self told me you've got it right. I can hear it in my mind, loudly. "This is so," or, "So be it," or, "Amen." I've heard this voice for years. Many, many years! But I can't do what either you or George just did, and I never said I could, young lady. You both presumed I could from day one. I taught you to use your minds. Your individual talents and dissimilar minds."

No one said anything until they reached Tumut. They all had different things on their miscellaneous minds.

Fancy Teddy Willis teaching us things he himself can't do, Barnard thought. How cool, how excellent is he? I always believed he was nearly perfect in every way. Surely a Saint, and almost a God.

Ted Willis knew of the existence of the Eleven-Eleven Spirit Guardians of the Halfway Realm and of their close association with Seraphim. Although the professor understood the Guardians to be occupying various facets of time within the space occupied by common mortals, he was always vague about their specific function. Ted often referred to them as "keeping universal balance." He called them the Voices of Joan of Arc, the Guides of Dante, or the Teachers of Nostradamus. But Ted knew none of them by their looks, name, code, or number.

George Barnard saw experiential evolutionary life as progressive according to a boldly sketched, eternity-foreseen blueprint. This blueprint could be little more than a rough outline of slow creature progress since the non-negotiable free will of fickle mortals could have a horrific impact on human advancement.

Accidents of space might "collide" with the flow of required events in time. Key individuals might be lost from that giant chessboard of life. Essential events might not come about to complete one of many successive time/space schemes in the overall strategy of guided evolution.

As a spare-time mortal rookie in a platoon of Spirit Guardians, Barnard followed orders, mostly, as instructed by the brilliantly minded Eleven-Eleven. In turn, the Guardians took their instructions from yet infinitely greater minds. And only the events that were most threatening to human welfare were circumvented by the Guardians. Only rarely was the mortal actually involved.

This was one of those occasions.

Louise Hewitt, Barnard suggests, might have long ago decided to care for her patients without relying on the advice of her real or imaginary Spirit Guide, John. Louise, for a time, continued to mistakenly see the event of the "Car at the Lake" as coercion by the Guardians.

The mother of two refused to acknowledge the function of the 11:11 Spirit Guardians as Protectors and Teachers, trustworthy and ethical in their ways. Her time had not yet come, but she, too, would soon "climb that rope, up into the sky, to meet the Great Biami". Barnard had sensed it, and probably, so had Professor Willis.

But Ted would never mention it.

Always

Will You care for my body whilst I am gone?
Will You see to its safe-keeping till I am through?
Then carry me to where I long to be,
  in ecstasy, always.

Let your helpers lift me high.
Bound and handcuffed, let me sleep and travel far,
  in that Golden Chariot of Light,
  to an Abode like no other.

Let me see what eyes cannot perceive.
Let me taste the pure nectar of Your Realm.
Let me listen to what ears cannot hear,
  sweet music divine.

Then take me back home,
  since I have more living to do.
But when You call me, I shall be there for You
  as You have been there for me,

  always

part six

The Golden Glow

At just twenty-seven years of age, Barnard had already been running his little company for more than six years. It was still growing rapidly. Production oversight, the construction of machinery and cameras, jigs and furniture for his firm's domestic use was foremost in his mind. He loved his job. Becoming a healer was the last thing this technical man would ever consider.

The sudden and unexpected arrival of the Great Master's Golden Glow, a Light that enveloped and illuminated both George's body and his clothes, was the turning point at which his life changed. It changed rapidly and drastically in those four short hours of his being wrapped in the Golden Glow.

The young businessman had no idea of what was happening to him. The Light brought sublime ecstasy, super-minded insight into the purpose of all evolutionary creatures of the time/space creations, boundless energy, and a feeling of oneness with all humankind. But it also frightened the wits out of him and troubled his eyesight for a number of days.

Since childhood, George Mathieu had been hearing inner voices, sometimes loudly expressed opinions. This was hardly considered to be a mentally hygienic phenomenon by either himself or anyone else. The disembodied voice episodes brought to mind the frightening specter of future, possibly violent schizophrenic episodes wrecking his life.

But how could he be so insane if he was so successful? And why were the voices not inviting him to kill or maim himself or others? If they did, that would surely be an indication that hard work, lots of worries and responsibilities were making him lose his marbles. The voices did nothing of the kind.

Again and again they came at appropriate moments and contained good advice or timely warnings. On very rare occasions, there would be a concise answer to a searching question that was on his mind.

Barnard suspected they were Spirit Guardians, Angels, or helpful but lost souls of the long ago departed, but he could never be sure. And that persistent feeling of doubt about his possibly, slowly losing the plot remained. He was human. Fear of the unknown was both an innate and a learned behavior.

Once or twice per week, at times much more often, he would awaken during the night, and at precisely eleven minutes past eleven. This went on for years. Mysterious as these occurrences seemed to be, they never bothered him. He would instantly go back to sleep, and sleep well.

"It's just that I constantly have so much damned work on my plate," Barnard explained to all who wanted to hear, "that I am perpetually thinking ahead of myself. Forty-nine minutes to be exact. What? Doesn't everyone else wake up at precisely midnight? You don't? Heavens! Go see your doctor and get a complete physical."

It would be still half a decade before he finally set eyes on the 11:11 of the Halfway Realm, to be told by his immediate Spirit Superior, "I am one thousand, one hundred and eleven. The name of our number, the number of our name." Finally, there was a connection between the voices and the wake-up calls. Either that, or George Mathieu had possibly spilled yet another dozen marbles.

But the experience of the Great Master's Golden Glow was not in the arena of things to be poked fun at. When the hype and ecstasy, the wonder of it all, wore off, the event was quickly banished to the deepest recesses of his mind and for a number of years. Despite his having become intuitively much sharper, as well as totally immune to colds and flu that were doing the rounds, Barnard was hiding. He had become a freak, even in his own eyes.

An indisputable connection between the years-long vocal contact with the Guardians and the happening of the Golden Glow was never proven in Barnard's mind, though it seemed likely there was a connection. The Golden Glow had to be associated with some greater ability to communicate with the Guardians, he felt. But the rookie of the Guardians' platoon would always long hesitate before discussing any of his illumination events.

Inevitably, raised eyebrows, scorn, or even threats, were the responses he got in a world where so many average people closed their minds to the wonders all around them.

21

"Biami's" Twins

There should be some way to stop the world from turning, just for a while. All those who have bitten off more than they can chew could feverishly catch up with neglected tasks. All well-organized citizens could take a break, spend an hour in the sauna, play with the children, have a siesta, or that extra game of tennis.

Perhaps planetary life was never meant to be a stepping stone to organization, balance and perfection, just an opportunity to occasionally minimize the inevitable chaos we create, Barnard considered.

The Associated Suppliers' project had come and gone. Once again, the firm's amount of work-in-progress was awesome. The number of patients being treated was also greater than usual. Barnard was fatigued, even moody at times.

With so many varied duties, George Mathieu knew his social life was often neglected. Someone in particular had been on his mind for days. He would telephone his old study comrade, Louise Hewitt, that evening.

She might be pregnant and wanting to tell him. They were close friends, still, but far apart. Perhaps she is in some kind of financial trouble, Barnard mused. Overextended as always. No. No. Louise would be pregnant. He could almost feel her presence.

"Tonight, Lou Lou. I shall definitely remember to call you," he muttered. And boy or girl, I implore you to name this new arrival after me. Georgette?

Less than an hour later, he lazily reached for his noisy telephone extension and grunted, "Yah! Workroom."

"It's Louise, George," said a jubilant voice on the telephone. "I'm so glad I caught you at work. I've got beautiful news. Brilliant news! Guess what."

"Guess what?" Barnard asked. Then, teasing, "You're pregnant! What else do you do? That'll make three, Louise. You must call this one after me. Congratulations! I'm sure you still don't know what causes it. When will you figure that out, girl?"

"No, I'm not pregnant! And you'll never guess this one, ever," she answered. She giggled like child. "I was visited by a Light!"

"This call is going to cost you a fortune, Lou Lou, in business hours," Barnard suggested. "Call me tonight at home, if it's a long story. I was actually going to give you a call tonight."

"Who cares about the cost?" she asked. "This is much too important to wait any longer. You've got to know. I'll tell you. I'll tell you now."

She sounded a bit like that emotional and excitable university student George Mathieu used to know when PMT made her life a total misery. That was ten years back down the track. Louise was married now, with two children, and running a busy private clinic. This was unusual behavior for her.

"Are you high on something?" Barnard asked tongue in cheek.

"You bet I am!" was the answer. "We are soaring! Annette and I—Annette's my friend—we were playing cards last night. We play lots of cards, once a week at least. And late last night, after midnight, we both reached for the same card. It was in the middle of the table, and we both went for it at the same time. And our arms got stuck! In mid-air! Our forearms were parallel, some two, or three inches apart, stuck fast in mid-air, and with a light all around them! It felt fantastic! We weren't a bit scared. What do you think of that?" she asked.

"I think congratulations are in order, Lou Lou. You lucky thing, you! Both of you have become Biami's children. Twins! Two for the price of one," Barnard told her, "how novel! Efficient. This universe must be hotting up."

"What does it mean?" she asked. "If you know what it means, you've gotta tell me! Did an angel or something visit us? Annette wants to know, too. She's here with me now. She says she knows it was an angel. Was it?"

Barnard needed to consider the strong feelings of Louise's friend. "What does your friend do for a living?" he asked.

"Community work," was the reply. "Heaps of it. We often handle cases together. Why do you want to know that?"

He ignored her question. "Both your accounts are well into the black, Louise," he explained. "What happened to you last night, in my view, was your taking delivery of a new and additional mind endowment. Both of you should find yourself becoming more intuitive, more intelligent really, and spiritually promoted. But I can't tell you if an angel delivered the package. Nobody knows how it works exactly." He hesitated, but only for a moment. "God Himself probably has a fairly good idea, but I don't," he joked. "So, Annette may well be right. Tell her to go with her intuition. You two are a pair of lucky little critters, believe me."

"George, is that what people mean by enlightenment, illumination, what happened to us?" she wanted to know.

"You could say something like that, Louise," he answered vaguely.

"What do you call it then?" she asked.

"I call it the Golden Glow, the Great Master's Golden Glow. I've seen it a number of times, Louise. Don't be alarmed if from now on it occasionally happens to one of your patients in your presence. If it does, it means you are temporarily occupying the place of a fully-fledged yogi, which you are not. But take it for granted he, or she—your patient, that is—is either very deserving, or in great need, desperate need, perhaps at a crossroads. In a sense, each of you has become somewhat of a yogi."

Louise hesitated for an instant. "George, I told Annette last night that I would ring you early this morning to ask you if you knew. And she said, "He knows. Oh, yes, he knows." What do you think of that?"

"A new mind endowment, Louise. Heightened intuition, like I told you," Barnard repeated.

"Is that what happened to you?" she asked.

"Perhaps something like it," he answered carefully, "on a number of occasions. Different each time. But unlike you two, I wasn't pregnant when it happened, Lou Lou." He tried hard not to laugh.

"Neither are we!" she shouted. "But we're stoked! High as kites about it. It felt so go-o-od! Oh, Annette says thank you. We want to come and see you, and talk about it with you," Louise suggested, "and stay for a whole month!"

"Don't," he told her. "You'll be hyped up like this for days. Don't do anything rash, anything much, meditate until you've settled down. I'll send you some stuff in the mail. And besides, Louise, I don't know that much about it anyway. The experience is very personal, for the Spirit Self and the soul, not so much the mind. That's why you, yourselves are a bit vague on it all. Give yourselves time to calm down. After that you'll do wonders."

"Okay," she answered, "if you say so. But you must tell me something else. No fibs or jokes now. You and Teddy Willis were talking about meeting that somebody called Biami, remember? When we did that trip to Tumut."

"Climbing the rope to meet up with Biami in the sky. Yes," he answered. "That's only a metaphor, a shaman's experience."

"What is that then?" she asked. "Not secret men's business, eh, eh, eh?"

"Talk to the wise ones amongst your indigenous patients, Louise," Barnard suggested, "rationally, please. They will give you a wonderful description of it."

Suddenly he felt utterly inadequate in carrying on with explaining it all to them in their ecstatic state. There had been experiences of many kinds for him. Sometimes they had involved his patients, as well as their therapist. More than anything he felt inhibited. A sharp intellect, or a freak? A psychic, or insane? From whose point of view?

Then there were those voices. At least, Ted Willis knew where his answers came from. He attributed them all to his Spirit Self. Bloody lucky Ted!

Barnard had his Teachers, the Spirit Guardians. But there had been other voices that never introduced their Owners. Just how many of these originated from Barnard's own Spirit Self, the rookie would never know. "You come to learn many things, very fast," ABC-22 had told him. "You are not a Specialist."

"You come to teach me many things, very fast," the Guardians' apprentice muttered mockingly under his breath, "and you've managed to utterly confuse me, Bzutu. A Jack of all trades you wanted; a master of none you have."

"Did you say something, George," Louise asked. "No secrets now, Boyo!"

"I was thinking, Louise." Barnard answered. "I was thinking you might write down your impressions of the event. You and Annette, both, but separately. Do it today. And you must send a copy of them to Teddy Willis. That will make his day." He paused. "Send me them, too, Louise, whilst you're on that high."

"Good as done! And we will always love you!" There was laughter. Then another bout of giggling from both women, and then the line went dead.

Louise would be inebriated with the "Great Master's Golden Glow" for the next two days at least. Annette likewise. Then the hype would wear off and Biami's Twins would become more productive, morally attuned, and spiritually enriched than ever.

Just One Regret . . .

Had he more quickly realized just who they were,
he would have shown them more respect.

Had he tried harder to fathom their brilliant minds,
he would have taken more of their teachings to heart.

Had he more clearly understood the purpose of their
being,
he would have more vigorously tried to assist them.

They were truly honorable.
He was sadly prejudiced.

They were exceedingly well informed.
He was grossly ignorant.

They were totally indefatigable.
He so often, and so quickly, gave up.

Still, for many years there was a strong celestial-mortal
alliance between the Eleven-Eleven of the Halfway
Realm,
their Seraphic Associates, and their flesh-and-blood
friend,
a common mortal.

Much was accomplished, many profited, and
there is just one regret . . .

They could have achieved so much more.

Epilogue

For almost ten more years, the Spirit Guardians" understudy, George Mathieu Barnard, did the Eleven-Eleven's bidding. Then he sold his business interests and retired to a country farm. Although he continued to practice as an occasional clinical hypnotherapist in his new environment, he soon became restless again. He sought out near-bankrupt and bankrupt companies to reorganize, re-finance and inject with new vigor. He quickly felt like he had never been so alive. He loved the challenges of repairing what most people saw as doomed companies.

Amazingly, at this time the Celestial / Mortal Alliance became more active than it had ever been. With a thorough knowledge of future events, Barnard was doing things that made little sense to others. Yet, each time his hunches turned out to be right, and people started to talk about him doing miracles. It couldn't last. People began to distrust the oddball troubleshooter who seemed to know their every thought before they were thinking it.

On one of his company rescue projects the rookie was beaten senseless. It happened so fast that not even the Spirit Guardians could come to his assistance in time. They arrived just seconds too late. Barnard took almost ten years to recover from the physical abuse. During that time there was relatively little contact with the Spirit Guardians of the Halfway Realm, only pain, confusion and despair. But as he slowly healed, he discovered a new way of contacting them. He suggested it, tested it extensively, and found his Superiors had accepted it. The ancient Guardians never turned their backs on the mortal veteran of so many years.

Barnard had been adopted for life.

The 11:11 Documents

In the Service of 11:11 is the second in a series of spiritual books that comprises the 11:11 Documents. The first book in this series called **The Search for 11:11** has been reprinted a number of times. Another popular major work is Lytske's **The Guiding Light Within,** and George's **The Anatomy of the Halfway Realm** – A Spirit Guardian's student's handbook.

In further volumes, George Barnard continues the story of his personal experiences – and treasured adventures of others who are working in cooperation with the Celestial / Mortal Alliance.

Written but not yet published are **By the Grace of 11:11** by George Barnard, and **Celestial Lessons** by Lytske.

Next in the Series

By the Grace of 11:11 – next to be published.

From as early as 1946, the Spirit Guardians took the opportunity to test George's diligence at some simple tasks. When the boy's father discovered one of these projects, the youngster owned up to having been directed by the Guardians. The ensuing conflict between father and son proved to be important for George to later remember his early association with the Guardians as they returned to guide him in business and in his clinical work.

After he recovered from his injuries sustained during a 1987 assault, contact with the elusive Guardians was re-established, and the Celestial / Mortal Alliance saved many from a threatening, fiery death. This exciting book in the series of 11:11 publications documents many amazing experiences of the 11:11 Emergency Platoon.

11:11 Services

We invite you to visit the 11:11 websites and message board at

www.1111progressgroup.com
www.1111angels.com
http://board.1111angels.com

and review the archived transcripts of celestial contact with George and other receivers of celestial messages. You may also provide your email address for inclusion on the 11:11 International Progress List which each week sends out some four or five transcripts of recorded contact with various Spirit Guides, Angels, and other Celestial Teachers.

The Akashic Construct

A guided meditation / visualization CD is available to facilitate your spiritual pursuits. It can be found on:

www.1111akashicconstruct.com

Are you one of many favored mortals who are also receiving the 11:11 spiritual wake-up calls? Perhaps you frequently note other double digit prompts, like 1:11, 12:12, or 22:22, even 12:34? We would like to hear from you.

Please contact us via our websites.